DATE DUE

APR 2 0 2015	
MAY 0 4 2015	

UNDERSTANDING ONLINE PIRACY

UNDERSTANDING ONLINE PIRACY

The Truth about Illegal File Sharing

Nathan W. Fisk

PRAEGER

An Imprint of ABC-CLIO, LLC

A B C CLIO

Santa Barbara, California • Denver, Colorado • Oxford, England

Copyright 2009 by Nathan W. Fisk

Library of Congress Cataloging-in-Publication Data
Fisk, Nathan W.
    Understanding online piracy : the truth about illegal file sharing / Nathan W. Fisk.
        p. cm.
    Includes bibliographical references and index.
    ISBN 978-0-313-35473-1 (alk. paper) — ISBN 978-0-313-35474-8 (ebook)
    1. Computer crimes—United States.   2. Copyright and electronic data processing—
United States.   3. Internet—Government policy—United States.   I. Title.
    HV6773.2.F58   2009
    364.16'62—dc22   2009009846

13   12   11   10   09   1   2   3   4   5

This book is also available on the World Wide Web as an eBook.
Visit www.abc-clio.com for details.

ABC-CLIO, LLC
130 Cremona Drive, P.O. Box 1911
Santa Barbara, California 93116-1911

This book is printed on acid-free paper ∞
Manufactured in the United States of America

To Sam, who got me into this,
To Liz, who got me through it,
and
To those in the STS Grad Lounge
who cheered me on the entire way.

Special thanks to Gareth Edel, for all of the stylish illustrations.

CONTENTS

1. Introduction   1

2. The History of Online Piracy   9

3. P2P Technologies and the Warez Scene   29

4. Managing P2P Risk   53

5. Extent and Effects of Online Piracy   75

6. Digital Copyright Law   101

7. Case Studies   121

8. The Future of File Sharing   137

Appendix A: Full Interview Transcripts   *153*

Appendix B: Resources and Information   *161*

Appendix C: Online Piracy Timeline   *165*

Notes   *169*

Glossary   *177*

Bibliography   *181*

Index   *187*

About the Author   *191*

Chapter 1

INTRODUCTION

Stop for a moment and think about what comes to mind when you encounter the term *online piracy*. Do you imagine a college student being sued by the suits in the intellectual property industry? A socially inept teenager in a darkened room illegally sharing files with the computer underground? Someone moving files onto his iPod? You may not consider yourself an expert, but your basic understanding of online piracy probably has at least something to do with your decision to read this book. The examples I just gave are somewhat stereotypical, but each fits with various commonly held representations of online piracy. On the basis of the stories commonly provided to us by the popular media, millions of pirates operate online, stealing billions of dollars' worth of digital content every year and being slowly picked off one by one through industry lawsuits. For most, online piracy, as defined by these types of popular representations, is detailed enough. As a reader of this book, it stands to reason that you are looking for a little more information to fill the gaps between the stories you might have heard from the news media or school administrators. What is online piracy? How can you protect yourself online? How much piracy goes on out there? What are the financial effects of piracy? Why is it illegal? Why does anyone do it at all? In this book, I hope to answer these questions by providing students and families with a rough guide to online piracy and digital copyright. Beyond these questions, there is something of a bigger picture, which most popular representations barely touch. An important struggle for control is being waged on the basis of online piracy, one that is constantly changing and shaping the ways in which we consume and create media. Now, this may be at least a little out of the scope of what every family needs to know, but my goal is to give you at least a sense of some of the deeper and more complex technical, legal, and social issues that intersect with online piracy as we know it.

ABOUT THE AUTHOR

Before we dive into what exactly online piracy is, and why it is important to discuss, I should probably tell you a little about myself, your native guide to one of the Internet's many gray areas. I've spent the last 15 years using computers and the Internet in various capacities, and like many others of my generation, I stumbled on the computer underground at a young age. From my first encounter—a private chat room on America Online.—I developed an interest in what was going on but never truly became anything more than an observer. I started my undergraduate work in information technology at the Rochester Institute of Technology (RIT) in autumn 1999, where I met and became close friends with many members of the warez, or online piracy scene. During this time, I became an active peer-to-peer (P2P) user, along with nearly every other college student in the nation, through the rise and fall of Napster in 2000 and 2001. My interest in the computer underground persisted, and nearing the completion of my degree, I found myself entering the world of computer crime research, alongside Dr. Samuel McQuade. Dr. McQuade and I worked on a number of computer crime research projects together, all of which measured online piracy in some way. Our research caught the attention of the Recording Industry Association of America (RIAA), and we were invited to present our findings to their top executives. From teenage pirate to presenter of research at RIAA headquarters, I like to think I have been fortunate enough to examine the phenomenon of online piracy from a variety of perspectives. That said, my history tends to shift my views closer to the consumer/pirate side of online piracy issues. Though I will be doing my best to push those views aside, I encourage you to do what you can to think critically about the information I present in this book, rather than merely taking what I say here as the final word of an online piracy expert. If, at times, you find yourself shaking your head and disagreeing with me (or others whose works I present here), then all the better.

WHAT IS ONLINE PIRACY?

The term *online piracy* is thrown around quite a bit, but what does it really mean? After all, we need some kind of definition, particularly when it comes to activities that may involve some form of legal penalty. We wouldn't want the Federal Bureau of Investigation (FBI) knocking on our door merely for loaning a DVD to a friend, nor would we want the movie studio that produced the DVD to go bankrupt because the world has opted to copy and share the film, rather than purchase it. As it turns out, online piracy is a broad category that encompasses a variety of different activities but provides little by way of clearly definable boundaries. As you'll see in Chapter 5, this quickly becomes apparent when looking at the research being done on online or digital piracy—even scientists doing the research struggle to develop meaningful and accurate definitions. Defining any new term is an extremely difficult task—as a society, we collectively give meaning to terms by using them in communication and invisibly negotiating their meanings—so pinning down any clear definition can be difficult. Luckily for us, we do have some historical information to help us with this definition. At least half the term—*piracy*—has been around for a long time.

Exactly when and where the term *piracy* was coined is not entirely clear, but the term has been in common use far longer than most people realize. The term dates to the late 1600s, only a few decades prior to the enactment of what is commonly viewed as the first copyright law. Historian Adrian Johns attributed the term *piracy,* as applied to copyright, to John Fell, then bishop of Oxford, who used the term in part to imply that the act of unauthorized copying of printed materials was in some way akin to the pillaging and rape in which seafaring pirates engaged.[1] The term originally carried a specific meaning, describing a book printer who printed a title that belonged to another printer without prior authorization, but eventually, the term came to be used to describe a broad range of dishonest behaviors within the printing community. Through the years, as additional forms of communication media and copying technologies were developed, the term continued to be used to describe the unauthorized copying and distribution of someone's work. Implicit in the use of the term *piracy* is the concept that the result of creative work has value and that individuals may somehow own or have the rights to control this work as they see fit—that the result of intangible *intellectual* work can be *property*.[2] In other words, piracy occurs when intellectual property is copied and distributed without the authorization of the person or organization that owns, or holds the rights to, the property.

When we start with such a definition, then defining *online* piracy becomes significantly easier. If *piracy* is the act of copying and distributing intellectual property without authorization from the rights holder, then *online piracy* is any act of piracy that uses computer networks as a mechanism for copying and distributing. At a number of points in this book, I'll be describing other, similar forms of piracy, so for clarification, I'll describe those forms here as well. More broadly than *online piracy,* I will use the term *digital piracy* with some frequency, particularly in Chapter 2. By *digital piracy,* I refer specifically to the piracy of digital media content, which can include anything from illegally copying (now ancient) software on punch cards to copying a DVD, but does not necessarily involve a computer network for distribution. In summary, *digital piracy* is a reference to the piracy of a specific type of *content* (like music piracy or movie piracy), whereas *online piracy* is a reference to a specific type of *distribution method.*

THE IMPORTANCE OF ONLINE PIRACY

Online piracy, digital piracy—what makes all this important enough that every family should know a little something about it? Well, it's obviously important enough for you to have picked up this book and read this far, so that in itself says something. What makes this topic important enough for you to read about it? Many would cite the drop in recording industry profits that are commonly associated with the activities of online pirates. This association has not been lost on the mainstream media, which have deemed online piracy important enough to cover with some frequency throughout the past two decades, regularly referencing millions of users[3] and billions of dollars in lost sales.[4] Other readers might cite the near-constant barrage of lawsuits brought by the recording industry against individual P2P users, another favorite topic of the mainstream media.[5] In their book *Pirates of the Digital Millennium,* Gantz and Rochester outline seven separate camps of individuals who have some kind of stake in online piracy and digital media content[6]:

1. Media trade organizations (e.g., RIAA, Motion Picture Association of America, Business Software Alliance)
2. Media content creators (e.g., Sony, Disney)
3. Device manufacturers/software developers (e.g., Microsoft, Apple)

4. Internet service providers (e.g., Comcast, Time Warner)
5. Governments and courts
6. Critics and scholars
7. Media consumers

Each of these (often overlapping) groups plays some significant role in facilitating and regulating online piracy. Depending on the situation at hand, they frequently find themselves either working together or at odds with one another on the battlefield of digital content and online piracy. These camps include extremely powerful organizations with billions of dollars in financial assets and encompass millions of people around the world. Online piracy isn't simply about people copying a few songs through the Internet; rather, it has significant implications for how we consume and produce media as a culture—which is one of many reasons why all these groups are struggling for control. Hidden in the very concept of online piracy are assumptions about creative content as property and who may use which content for what purposes. As cultures around the world increasingly utilize forms of digital media for entertainment, education, and artistry, efforts to manage online piracy simultaneously regulate the means by which these cultures reproduce themselves. As an issue potentially involving millions of people, billions of dollars, some of the most powerful organizations of our time, and the means of cultural consumption and production, online piracy is certainly worth thinking and talking about.

WHAT IS COVERED IN THIS BOOK?

What is it that you can expect to read in the remainder of this book? Online piracy is undeniably a global phenomenon, affecting the intellectual property industries in countries around the world. In this book, however, I'll be focusing primarily on the United States for a number of reasons: first, the intellectual property industry in the United States is among the largest in the world and, to a certain extent, has the most to lose from any potentially negative effects of online piracy; second, the history of online piracy, including the construction of both the technologies and the cultures that facilitate online piracy, has been traditionally based in the United States; finally, navigating global copyright law is an extremely complex task as every country manages copyright violations in different ways—covering the ways in which online piracy is managed across the world could easily fill a number of books. Though I may occasionally describe some of the ways in which copyright laws conflict with online piracy in different countries, the focus will primarily be on U.S. copyright law. Speaking of the law, I would like to make one point perfectly clear from the beginning: I am not a lawyer, and I am not providing legal advice in this work. There will, of course, be sections in which I describe the workings of the law as it pertains to online piracy and digital copyright, along with sections in which I discuss the use of various technologies that might be used to violate copyright law; however, I present all of the material in this book as information, not as legal advice. I imagine that even if you find yourself in legal trouble, telling the judge that "the redheaded guy who wrote that piracy book told me to do it" won't get you very far; therefore, if you need legal advice, find a lawyer.

Here in Chapter 1, I've attempted to provide a quick introduction to the concept of online piracy and the challenges involved in creating definitional boundaries around any potentially illegal activity. It is hoped that at this point in the chapter, you also have a sense of the cultural relevance of online piracy, in addition to having gained at least some understanding of the parties that have something at stake in the world of online piracy.

In Chapter 2, I'll be starting out with a history of online piracy and P2P networking. P2P is a relatively recent phenomenon, but the trajectory of online piracy can be traced much further into the past. Piracy has evolved alongside the development of the personal computer: the first documented case of digital piracy was recorded in the 1970s. From there, I describe the pirate bulletin board systems of the 1980s, the FTP and Internet Relay Chat (IRC) sites of the 1990s, and finally, the ways in which these historical influences came to shape the development and resulting popularity of Napster, the first widely used P2P network.

Chapter 3 covers the technologies that facilitate online piracy, focusing primarily on various P2P networks. As it turns out, the very design of these networks has a lot to do with how they have been treated by the intellectual property industry, the courts, and Internet service providers. Of course, not everyone is an information technology wizard, so Chapter 3 starts with a crash course in the basics of computer networking: TCP/IP. If you're generally a technophobe, fear not—networking is not nearly as complicated as you might think. In addition to the technical inner workings of the Internet and P2P, I also discuss where the content available on P2P networks originates. Of course, the users of P2P networks share with each other, but the majority of content originally comes from a more organized community of online pirates, collectively known as the *warez scene.* These pirates are highly organized and are responsible for the prerelease content commonly found on P2P networks, including music, movies, and software.

Using P2P networks for file sharing, regardless of whether or not the content is copyrighted, carries along with it certain risks. Chapter 4 defines these risks, from malware to the unwanted disclosure of private information—an increasing concern for government networks. Of course, those users who download and share copyrighted works online face other, more specific risks from the intellectual property industry. I describe the methods used by the recording and movie industries to gather evidence against and identify P2P users. Closing the chapter, I provide information on how to mitigate all the risks associated with P2P use, including those faced by users who choose to violate copyright. Chapter 4 additionally includes a segment specifically for parents, describing methods to determine if children in your home are using P2P networks to download copyrighted content, and what to do about it.

Online piracy is a term that masks a broad variety of activities, making it extremely difficult to examine in a systematic way. Chapter 5 is a summary of research that has been done on the nature and extent of online piracy, starting with early studies by some of the first computer crime researchers. Despite the fact that online piracy has been a concern for both the intellectual property industry and the government for decades, relatively little research has been completed on the topic. Additionally, many of the stories told by the studies conflict with one another, resulting in an unclear picture of how many people are engaged in online piracy regularly and the effects piracy actually has on the intellectual property industry.

In Chapter 6, I discuss the various laws that regulate and define online piracy and the penalties associated with violating these laws. First, I once again return to the past, providing a history of copyright law starting with the invention of the printing press. Though the printing press may seem somewhat antiquated for a discussion on online piracy, the laws that were developed in the wake of its introduction form the basis of our copyright laws today. Additionally, a number of interesting parallels exist between early printing pirates and the online pirates of today. Following that history, I describe in detail what copyright law means for Internet and P2P users and how copyright law is used in court against those accused of digital copyright violations.

Providing a more detailed look at how the law works in practice is Chapter 7, which contains a number of case studies. I begin with some of my own personal experiences on the campus of RIT during the Operation

Buccaneer raids by the U.S. Customs Agency and FBI in December 2001 as an example of a criminal piracy case. Then I describe two separate civil copyright cases: a typical case, in which the defendant chose to settle with the copyright holder, and a case brought to court and won by the defendant. The first case study describes the RIAA settlement process, whereas the second describes the actions of the RIAA in court. Finally, I describe the case of *A&M Records v. Napster,* the court battle that forced Napster off the Internet.

I conclude the book with Chapter 8, in which I discuss recent developments in technology, law, and business that have the potential to shift the course of online piracy in the future. For each development, I briefly attempt to predict how the development will shape the future of online piracy, and I ultimately conclude that despite the growing number of users flocking to P2P networks, the future is not entirely bright for pirates worldwide.

In the appendices, you will find a variety of supplemental resources. Appendix A contains the full transcripts of the two interviews conducted for this book: the first with a student who was targeted for legal action by the RIAA, and the second with a member of the warez scene. Appendix B contains a brief list of Web pages and additional readings that will be of interest to those doing research on online piracy. Finally, Appendix C contains an online piracy timeline, which outlines the key historical moments described in this book.

Regardless of why or how you came across this book, it is my hope that you will find some useful information contained within its pages. If you belong to a family with children, I suggest you focus on chapters 3 and 4 to bring you up to speed on exactly what technologies are used for P2P and how to use such technologies safely. Teens and college students, who I imagine already know a little something about P2P networks, will likely be most interested chapters 4 and 7, to get some information about avoiding a lawsuit and what happens when a P2P user is targeted for legal action. For those using this text for research, Chapters 2 and 5 contain a variety of historical facts and statistics, which may be useful for further writing.

Chapter 2

THE HISTORY OF ONLINE PIRACY

> We didn't wake up one morning and the Internet was there . . . How did
> we get there? That's what you want to know about history for.
> —Steven Punter[1]

The copying of information is far from a new phenomenon. The technologies change, the people change, and the cultures change, but choose to examine any point in human history and you will invariably find people copying and distributing the work of others in some form. This is certainly not to say that copying is part of human nature or that copying is the right thing to do, but copying *is* in our past. Technologies that facilitate the production and distribution of information have heavily influenced the shape of history, most particularly when they have been accessible to larger populations of people. From the printing press to the recordable DVD, each technology has gotten us increasingly closer to the digital file sharing of today. Each has shaped the practice of copying and distributing information, and each has shaped the ways in which we think about copying and distributing information. Fittingly, in a brief presented by innovation scholars during the recent *MGM v. Grokster* case, it was noted that

> Very frequently, new technologies have a "dual-effect": they simultaneously
> are capable of substantial legitimate uses but also make exploitation of copy-
> righted works more difficult or costly for old business models. This was true
> of the printing press itself (the invention of which led to copyright as a legal

concept). It was true of virtually all new technology products in the analog Electronic Age (from telegraphy and photography, through telephony, the phonograph, the motion picture, radio, broadcast and cable television, the copy machine, and the VCR). And it has been a marked feature of the vibrant new technologies of the Digital Age.[2]

While it may come as some surprise, the same types of situations that have arisen following the widespread use of digital file-sharing networks can be observed following the adoption of other forms of copying and distribution technologies. One of the best comparisons comes from the impact that the printing press had on the sheet music industry in the early 1900s. At that time, England was facing a national piracy problem with sheet music—somewhat similar to the digital music piracy problem governments face today. Despite the creation of the Stationers' Guild, which tightly controlled the operation of printing presses, the number of illegal copies of sheet music being printed and sold was on the rise. Sheet music pirates would print out warehouses full of sheet music, which could then be sold at a significantly lower price on the British market. Legitimate printers were forced to compete with the pirates, with prices of pirated copies more than 90 percent lower than prices of legitimate copies. While early copyright law protected sheet music, the sheer volume of the problem made enforcement difficult for legitimate publishers. Publishers would often band together, organizing raids on the pirates to destroy illegitimate copies. Even after changes in the law made copyright infringement a criminal matter, police found it difficult to enforce the law in the face of overwhelming public support for the illegitimate printers.[3] The illegitimate printers were viewed by the public as a check on the music printing industry, preventing sheet music prices from being artificially inflated— which was a common practice for legitimate printers.[4] After all, where else could they legally purchase the sheet music they wanted?

For those of my readers who are even slightly aware of the ongoing battle between the recording industry (represented by the Recording Industry Association of America, RIAA) and online file sharers, at least some of the sheet music example should sound slightly familiar. As was mentioned in the extract from the *MGM v. Grokster* case, each innovative form of information copying or distribution system has led to other situations in which the intellectual property industry has fought to maintain its legally given rights, while publicly supported networks of illegitimate copiers distribute works at little to no cost. While the history of copying and the history of file sharing are inextricable, this is, after all, a book on *online piracy*, not copying in general. And we all know that online file sharing started with Napster, arguably the first and only file-sharing service to ever truly become a mainstream icon, so where better to start a history of digital file sharing?

On the campus of Northeastern University in autumn 1999, Shawn Fanning began to develop Napster, the software that would launch what became the first widely used peer-to-peer (P2P) file-sharing network in the world. After releasing Napster to a small group of about 30 friends—simply as a test of the software—use of Napster spread quickly, first to university campuses, and then to homes and businesses with high-bandwidth Internet connections. Despite the fact that the Napster network has since been shut down due to legal issues (we'll get to that in Chapter 7), Fanning forever changed the intellectual property industry. To this day, because Napster was initially designed for sharing music, file sharing is still primarily associated with music piracy. However, before we get too far ahead of ourselves, let's take a closer look at Napster and try to get a better understanding of why and how Fanning developed it.

According to Fanning, he was the sole developer of Napster, acting out of a desire to share music with his friends on campus. Well, as the innovation scholars writing for the *MGM v. Grokster* case pointed out, there were plenty of technologies capable of copying and distributing music available to Fanning—the printing press, the audio cassette, the compact disc—why not just use one of those? Fanning was part of a generation of students who both owned computers and had access to university networks, connecting them all together, and he believed that using those resources to share music was an acceptable and important practice. But the computers available to Fanning were not just any computers: they had the storage space necessary to store the comparatively large audio files, and they were fast enough to compress and decompress music in MP3 format, a task with which earlier computers would have struggled. Given that the computer itself played a role in how Fanning developed Napster, who developed the computer that Fanning used, and why? Did its developer take into consideration that increasing the capacity and processing power of personal computers may lead to copyright violation? And what about the network? It, too, played a role in Fanning's ability to develop Napster, providing a previously unavailable high-speed connection between students' computers. Who made the network possible, and how did its developer affect the development and adoption of Napster? Of course, we can't forget about the specific attitude toward file sharing that Fanning held—who and what led Fanning to believe that file sharing was an acceptable behavior? Who decided what computers and networks are, anyway?

Obviously, we could go on like this forever, placing Fanning and Napster in an ever expanding network of people and technologies, tracing the trajectory of Napster indefinitely through history. The point that I am trying to make here is that file-sharing technology, as with any other form of technology, did not simply pop into existence, free of external influence. New technologies are a result of an incredibly complex convergence of both social and technical influences, situated in a specific location and time. By following both the technologies and the social groups that facilitate file sharing as they co-construct each other through history, we should get a better sense of how file sharing has become such a widespread phenomenon. So then, if copying information is not a new phenomenon, and file sharing is older than Napster, where should we begin our history of file sharing? Where can we start to trace the trajectory of file sharing, across which both the technologies and the social factors that shape file sharing began to become visible? While there are arguably many periods through the history of computing that would make do as starting points, one stands out as a particularly appropriate place to begin: the first meeting of the Homebrew Computer Club. It was in the 1970s, in what would later become known as the Silicon Valley, that a group of amateur hackers and engineers began to hold meetings to discuss the development of computer hardware and software as a hobby. This moment was vital because it marked not only a technological revolution, but additionally, the founding of a culture of computer developers that continues to influence hardware and software even today. Simply by choosing to become involved in programming, Fanning took part in that culture, with its own language, ethics, and roles, which influenced the technologies he helped develop himself.

In the mid-1970s, the personal computer as we know it today was still a few years from being realized. Discussions about computers typically called to mind images of huge, room-sized mainframe computers, owned and maintained by massive corporations and research organizations, rather than the desktop and laptop computers that are called to mind today. Private, individual ownership of computers was extremely rare as few individuals could afford the incredibly high price and maintenance of such hulking machines. The very concept of a computer that one could own individually was a radical one, which is why they were referred to as personal computers, rather than just computers. The only personal computer on the market was Ed Roberts's Altair 8800, available through a mail order kit. This kit required buyers to solder all of the components together themselves to get a functional computer, with 24 switches used for input and a display consisting of a series of blinking red lights. Obviously, it took considerable technical skill to assemble the kit, and anyone attempting to construct a computer at the time (with or without the official kit) typically met with some form of problem, requiring the assistance of others. Hobbyist groups and clubs began to form across the nation as more people began to take interest in the Altair. Of these groups, the Homebrew Computer Club, in particular, is most frequently cited as having the most influence over the personal computer as we know it today. Inspired by the Altair, and the potential to bring people together using computers, two California engineers began to post flyers advertising the club in March 1975, offering discussion, assistance with projects and—most important—the free exchange of information.

The club was a success, and participation seemed to grow with each meeting. From the beginning, the free exchange of ideas in a collaborative environment was one of the main goals of the group. Stephen Levy describes the members discussing expectations at the first meeting of the club in his book *Hackers: Heroes of the Computer Revolution:* "They discussed what they wanted in a club, and the words people used most were 'cooperation' and 'sharing.'"[5] The concepts of cooperation, sharing, and accessibility were central to the core ethic that all the club members shared. Levy termed this unspoken code the *Hacker Ethic,* which "sublimated possession and selfishness in favor of the common good, which meant anything that could help people hack more efficiently."[6] These hackers were not the criminal, black-hat hackers commonly referred to today. Then, the term *hacker* referred to someone who treated working with computer hardware and software as a kind of art, emphasizing free and open access to any information that would enrich the learning environment. Club members would work tirelessly on their own projects, developing innovative hardware and software for the new computers, only to share their work openly at the meetings. This resulted in an explosion of growth for the newly created computers, as the Homebrew hackers created displays, keyboards, and various forms of software. All the hackers would help one another to recreate and modify the projects to fit their needs. Even corporate secrets were openly shared, and industry insiders would announce the most exciting gossip they could dig up, regardless of confidentiality issues. One member even managed to "acquire" prototype chips from Atari containing the software for Pong, trading the chips with other members for hardware.

Given the emphasis on free and open access to computer information, it comes to no surprise that the first recognized instances of digital piracy happened here. At this time, the majority of software written for personal computers was shared openly, and software developers were still unclear about the extent to which their creations were protected under copyright law—assuming that software copyright was even a consideration. On June 10, 1975, Bill Gates and Paul Allen held a demonstration of their newly developed Micro-Soft (now Microsoft) BASIC, a programming language for the MITS Altair. Included in the manual for Micro-Soft BASIC was a small warning that read, "Copying or otherwise distributing MITS software outside of the terms of such an [licensing] agreement may be a violation of copyright laws."[7] This statement represented one of the first software end user licensing agreements, making a claim that software can, and should, be protected under copyright law. Obviously, this ran contrary to the popular belief among the computer clubs and hobbyists. An unidentified attendant at this demonstration managed to steal one of the paper tape copies of the software. This copy eventually made its way to one of the Homebrew Computer Club moderators, who made 50 copies of the software for distribution to club members. However, each member who took a copy was asked to return to the next meeting with two to provide to other members. While the club was divided on the issue of continuing to copy and use the software, few members refused a copy. Bill Gates, in an attempt to prevent the copies from being distributed further, wrote a letter directly to the Homebrew Computer Club newsletter that described the copying of the paper tape as "stealing."[8] The use of the term *stealing* represented the differences between the ways in which the commercial developers and hobbyist developers understood software. For Gates, and the majority of early professional software developers outside of the hobbyist scene, software was "owned" by the developers, and as such, users only had license to use the software, not to make copies. To this day, the ideological debate between free software supporters and commercial developers continues.

Just as today, tinkering with computers could be an incredibly costly hobby, and many of the Homebrew members began selling the hardware and software they had developed. On placing ads in magazines and newspapers, these members found themselves inundated with orders. Eventually, the Homebrew Computer Club became fragmented into multiple startup

AN OPEN LETTER TO HOBBYISTS

by William Henry Gates III
February 3, 1976

To me, the most critical thing in the hobby market right now is the lack of good software courses, books and software itself. Without good software and an owner who understands programming, a hobby computer is wasted. Will quality software be written for the hobby market?

Almost a year ago, Paul Allen and myself, expecting the hobby market to expand, hired Monte Davidoff and developed Altair BASIC. Though the initial work took only two months, the three of us have spent most of the last year documenting, improving and adding features to BASIC. Now we have 4K, 8K, EXTENDED, ROM and DISK BASIC. The value of the computer time we have used exceeds $40,000.

The feedback we have gotten from the hundreds of people who say they are using BASIC has all been positive. Two surprising things are apparent, however, 1) Most of these "users" never bought BASIC (less than 10% of all Altair owners have bought BASIC), and 2) The amount of royalties we have received from sales to hobbyists makes the time spent on Altair BASIC worth less than $2 an hour.

Why is this? As the majority of hobbyists must be aware, most of you steal your software. Hardware must be paid for, but software is something to share. Who cares if the people who worked on it get paid?

Is this fair? One thing you don't do by stealing software is get back at MITS for some problem you may have had. MITS doesn't make money selling software. The royalty paid to us, the manual, the tape and the overhead make it a break-even operation. One thing you do do is prevent good software from being written. Who can afford to do professional work for nothing? What hobbyist can put 3-man years into programming, finding all bugs, documenting his product and distribute for free? The fact is, no one besides us has invested a lot of money in hobby software. We have written 6800 BASIC, and are writing 8080 APL and 6800 APL, but there is very little incentive to make this software available to hobbyists. Most directly, the thing you do is theft.

What about the guys who re-sell Altair BASIC, aren't they making money on hobby software? Yes, but those who have been reported to us may lose in the end. They are the ones who give hobbyists a bad name, and should be kicked out of any club meeting they show up at.

I would appreciate letters from any one who wants to pay up, or has a suggestion or comment. Just write to me at 1180 Alvarado SE, #114, Albuquerque, New Mexico, 87108. Nothing would please me more than being able to hire ten programmers and deluge the hobby market with good software.

Bill Gates

General Partner, Micro-Soft

companies, and many members became too busy with their own work to continue attending. Although many of these companies have since failed, many played critical roles as pioneers of the personal computer industry. Most notably, members Steve Jobs and Steve Wozniak went on to found Apple, the same company that eventually developed the iPod and iTunes. Despite the fact that the Homebrew Computer Club eventually disbanded, the hacker ethic that was cultivated now lives on even today among similar groups of technologically savvy hobbyists, programmers, and engineers, many of whom play a role in developing the information technologies that we use every day.

What does all of this have to do with Sean Fanning, Napster, and file sharing as we know it? At the Homebrew Computer Club, along with the other clubs like it spread across the nation, engineers and hobbyists helped to create the basis for the computers we use today. The design decisions made by Homebrew Computer Club members can still be seen in modern-day computers, and those decisions were based on the values and assumptions that they held—most important, the hacker ethic. As Homebrew Computer Club members went about developing the hardware and software for their own personal computers, they frequently did so with open access to information in mind. Technology that they developed continued to allow the user to share, tinker, and explore, making it possible for someone like Sean Fanning to develop a system like Napster. Furthermore, the same hacker ethic, which promoted free access to information and worked against preventing people from sharing copies of digital information (like MITS Altair BASIC), has traveled through the years and influenced a large number of other hobbyists and engineers who have a passion for information technologies—particularly college students enrolled in technical programs. Most important, however, the ethic shaped the form of personal computers as they were designed by hobbyists and engineers.[9]

As the Homebrew Computer Club had its first meeting, the Internet, too, was just getting its start. While the Internet, as an interconnection of multiple networks, did not yet exist, wide-scale networking was being developed as the ARPANET, a project funded by the Defense Advanced Research Projects Agency under the direction of Lawrence G. Roberts. Based off of research and memos by J.C.R. Licklider and Leonard Kleinrock, plans to develop the ARPANET were published by Roberts in 1967, and the first network connections were made between the Stamford Research Institute and the University of California, Los Angeles, in 1969. E-mail was introduced and immediately became a popular application among ARPANET users. From there, the ARPANET grew quickly. By 1975, the network had grown to include 57 different locations, just prior to being turned over to the U.S. Department of Defense. It was the largest, and the first, computer network at the time, but it was not yet accessible by the public. Because the major computer networks of the time comprised mainly mainframe computers, and because they generally were not accessible by the public, file sharing was still an activity that took place primarily through copying digital media and physically delivering it to others—just like the paper tape copies at the Homebrew Computer Club. This process is now somewhat jokingly referred to as sending files through the SneakerNet because files were actually walked from one computer to another. However, as interest in networking personal computers increased, the development of the electronic bulletin board system, or BBS, would provide new avenues for file sharing through direct connections between computers.

Bell Telephone developed the first modem in 1963, which allowed computers to connect to one another through telephone lines. However, it was not until 1977, when D. C. Hayes released a modem that could operate with a variety of different, unstandardized personal computers, that hobbyists began to purchase modems for personal use. Only two years later, the first BBS was placed online by Ward Christensen and Randy Suess on February 16, 1979, in Chicago, Illinois. Christensen and Suess were both members of a computer club, like the Homebrew Computer Club, known as the Chicago Area Computer Hobbyist's Exchange (CACHE). This first BBS, known as CBBS, was designed primarily to publish electronically the club newsletters and club information, in addition to providing a space for club members to share messages. Many users connecting to the CBBS had no computer monitor available to display the text received by the BBS, and instead relied on a printer, which would print each character as it came in on a spool of paper. As the board became increasingly popular, receiving calls from areas outside of Chicago, CACHE members began to distribute the BBS software Christensen had written, allowing others to modify the code and add features.

The number of boards increased as the software spread from hobbyist group to hobbyist group across the United States. While the original CBBS software was unable to store files or allow users to send private messages to one another, these features were developed by other hobbyist programmers. This first generation of BBS users and system administrators primarily comprised adult hobbyists, who had actively built their own computers either from kits or from scratch. Because of the sheer level of skill necessary to build a computer capable of connecting to boards, participation was limited. However, the personal computer market began to grow. Members of hobbyist computer clubs began forming their own companies to meet demand for hardware and software, and the larger companies, such as IBM, began marketing their own personal computers. Advertising campaigns were targeted heavily at parents and children, making the personal computer appear as both a powerful educational tool and a futuristic gaming machine. As these more accessible computers entered the market, a less savvy generation of computer users began to flock to the boards. Many of these new users were teenagers, who had either received computers as gifts or who had saved money for the purchase of a computer. Personal computers at that time were no small investment, and some teenagers actively chose to purchase a computer over a car simply to gain access to boards. The original hobbyists were displeased, to say the least, at having their private electronic messaging systems invaded. As Randy Suess describes in an account of BBS history, "You could buy a TRS-80, download your friend's software to it, and 'now I'm a BBS.' They didn't have to know a damn thing, all they had to do was have a phone line and they could say they were a sysop [system operator]. High schools were full of sysops!"[10] In a way, the boards represented the social networking sites of their time. In 1982, *Time* magazine named the computer "Machine of the Year," the first of only one of two times the Person of the Year award has been given to a nonhuman. One year later, in 1983, the movie *War-Games* was released in theaters. In one of the first scenes in the movie, the main character, played by Matthew Broderick, is shown using a personal computer and modem in an attempt to illegally access and download pre-release games from software developers.[11] News coverage of the exploits of the computer underground rose dramatically following the release of *WarGames,* further portraying hackers as powerful and mysterious. That year, the modem became a must-have Christmas item for thousands of teenagers across the United States.[12]

This younger generation of BBS users took a different approach toward computers: they were more interested in using the computers than they were in understanding the computers. Using the computers meant using software—software that could then be easily traded through boards. Many had also begun trading games through their own SneakerNets, borrowing and copying from friends and relatives. In the early 1980s, it was still unclear as to whether or not computer software was covered under copyright law, and even the technical experts in the hobbyist groups were conflicted on the issue—so for the new computer users, copyright was barely a consideration. It was acceptable to copy games and software, so everyone that could, did. Indeed, copying and trading games was an easy way for many young computer users to gain acceptance and status among their peers—and gaining access to boards made games even easier to obtain. As one BBS sysop remarked, "I used to copy and trade video games with my friends, which lead to one of my buddies saying 'Hey, do you know what a BBS is? You can get games for free!' . . . I mean, all I know is pirate boards."[13] You may at this point be wondering why these groups shared only software. Keep in mind that at this point, personal computers were generally incapable of displaying video of any sort, and audio was extremely limited—not to mention the fact that the bandwidth and storage space needed to transmit files of that size were unavailable. Simply put, because there were no computers powerful enough to actually create or store digital video or audio, there were no other types of files to share.

To an extent, computer games acted as a gateway into the computer underground for many young computer users.[14] For many, this was all that boards were useful for—simply to dial up and download software. Others, however, found something more: a community. Of course, the games and software that could be found on boards were put there by someone, and they were put there for the same reasons that people copied and shared software among friends outside of the BBS: for acceptance and status.[15] Some BBS users who started out downloading software began sharing and trading as well, congregating around boards that specialized in software piracy. Software developers had realized that their software was being copied and began to develop copy protection measures. These measures varied from requesting that users enter a word or phrase in the software manual to requiring users to enter a license key on installation. While these measures made copying more difficult for the average computer user, many of the BBS users saw copy protection as a challenge.

The software traders began devising ways to crack the copy protection measures built into software, allowing them to freely distribute working copies. Cracking became a complex game with thousands of competitors, as what is now known as the *warez* scene—slang for pirated software scene—grew. Software pirates used the boards to meet, form groups, and communicate, competing to release software onto the boards the fastest.

By 1985, it was estimated that there were approximately 4,000 boards in the United States, and these were increasingly run by nonhobbyist computer users.[16] After all, outside the cost of the computer and modem, which was steadily decreasing, an active BBS cost nothing to run. However, those who wished to dial in to boards were not so lucky. After all, dialing long-distance for hours on end to transfer software, communicate with group

FROM AN INTERVIEW WITH A WAREZ SCENE MEMBER

I started BBS Warez around 1993, trading games and BBS software and applications for DOS. After that I found out about the Internet and obtained a Netcom account (notable because they were one of the companies Kevin Mitnick hacked), and started using Usenet to get software. If I remember correctly this was in 1995. From Usenet I progressed to IRC and Web sites, I actually ran a small HPAVC [hacking, phreaking, anarchy, virus, cracking] site for a time. Eventually, I was hanging out in warez IRC channels on efnet and various private networks, trading files. I actually ended up writing my own software to automate the sharing of my collection.

That situation continued right up until I entered college in 1999, at which point I gained access to true high-bandwidth connections. I made some friends on campus with interests and was introduced to some members of the anime fansub group AVCD (anime video CD) on IRC. We quickly put together a server using spare parts and put it on the campus network. We ran a top-tier anime fansub distribution site, which gave us access to all sorts of other content.

members, and catch up on the latest scene news could get extremely expensive. Teenage pirates frequently found themselves in danger of losing their connection to the boards as their parents received phone bills totaling hundreds of dollars. For this reason, the links between pirate groups and other computer underground groups were very strong. In particular, the computer underground relied on the abilities of the *phreaks,* who systematically explored and exploited the telephone networks. Phreaks, who were also heavy BBS users, would discuss methods for fraudulently avoiding long-distance telephone charges and make calling card numbers available to those who needed them. Hackers,[17] who broke into and explored computer systems and networks, also played an important role in the warez scene, typically using their advanced skills to assist with software protection cracking. Many members of the computer underground wore many hats—pirating software, trading calling card numbers, and bragging about their latest exploits in the heart of some corporate computer system—all of which gained them more prestige and respect among the BBS communities. However, pirates were seen as one of the lower social castes of the computer underground, as hacking and phreaking required more skill and knowledge to perpetrate.

Between all of the illegal, or, at best, questionably legal, activities taking place on the boards and the media panic surrounding underground activities sparked by *WarGames,* it was not long before law enforcement officials began to take action. Of the estimated 4,000 boards available to BBS users in 1985, at least 3 were sting operations being run by local police officers.[18] Police officers and other federal law enforcement agents would pose as sysops, waiting for users to visit their boards looking to trade software, cards, or information. They would befriend the users, looking to gain access to other boards, many of which had exclusive elite sections known only to a select few, where particularly sensitive or illegal topics were discussed. Slowly, they would collect evidence against underground BBS users. However, during this time, law enforcement was not entirely interested in pirates; rather, they were interested in hackers and phreaks. During the late 1980s, fear over the power that these groups held was spreading. While most of those with the power to accomplish such a feat would never do so, the mere fact that some BBS users had the *capability* to shut down the national telephone network had many officials extremely concerned. One notable member of the Legion of Doom, a notorious hacking group active through the 1980s and 1990s, mentioned—during an interrogation by the Secret Service—that it was possible to crash the 911 system throughout the South. But because hackers, phreaks, and "warez d00ds" tended to congregate in the same online spaces, when law enforcement began seizing boards in search of evidence of telephone and credit card fraud, the warez scene was affected as well.

At the peak of BBS popularity, it was estimated that there were over 150,000 boards being operated in the United States alone.[19] Boards at that time represented the primary way for personal computer users to get online—despite the fact that being online meant something very different then than it does now. Boards acted as a social networking site, Web forum, and file-sharing service for the computer users of the time. Public Internet access, however, was still unavailable. The Internet—or at least significant segments of what eventually became the Internet—was governed by a set of rules known as the Acceptable Use Policy, or AUP. The AUP allowed the use of the Internet only for academic purposes, banning all commercial use. However, private, non-Internet network access was available through a number of service providers such as GEnie, CompuServe, Prodigy, and later, America Online (AOL). In 1989, the AUP restrictions were lifted, paving the way for the first true Internet service providers (ISPs). Rather than simply connecting to one other computer—as was the case with the boards—computer users with Internet access could connect to all of the computers, and computer users, connected to the network simultaneously. The lifting of the AUP restrictions also marked the beginning of the end for the BBS, but not the warez scene. While law enforcement officers were just beginning their assault on underground boards, the now publicly accessible Internet offered new opportunities for sharing copyrighted materials. Internet Relay Chat (IRC) and File Transfer Protocol (FTP), two technologies which were of limited use to software pirates under the AUP, now became powerful tools. FTP was formally standardized as an Internet protocol in 1985 and allowed computers to host and send files across TCP/IP (see Chapter 3) networks. IRC, as the name implies, was the first widely used form of Internet chat room, developed by Jarkko Oikarinen in 1988. The simple chat system grew more complex as developers added features and eventually allowed for the transfer of files through IRC. Combined, the two technologies allowed for easier and faster communication and distribution between pirate groups and storage servers. Rather than waiting as each individual user connected to a BBS one at a time, multiple Internet users could connect, chat, and transfer files with IRC and FTP. Additionally, FTP and IRC were generally unknown to law enforcement officials, who were then focusing attention on underground boards. As warez groups began using FTP and IRC more extensively, the warez scene split between the slowly fading boards and the Internet.

While IRC and FTP allowed for more efficient file sharing and group organization, public access to the Internet alone did not significantly change the warez scene. However, the introduction of one new technology generally unrelated to file transfer would indirectly act as a major force of change: the World Wide Web. In 1991, Tim Berners-Lee publicly announced the details of the World Wide Web project, and in 1993, Marc Andreessen released Mosaic, the first popular Web browser.[20] The Web was a near-immediate success, bringing the power to easily publish material on the Internet to a booming Internet population. In 1994, the major network service providers (CompuServe, AOL, GEnie, and Prodigy) began connecting their networks to the Internet, providing Internet and Web access to millions of existing customers. Additionally, hardware manufacturers were developing increasingly faster modems, allowing for higher-bandwidth connections to the Internet. The tables were turned on the BBS software pirates, many of whom were part of the wave of new users who unsettled computer hobbyists in 1983. Unlike the boards, IRC was open to the public, making warez groups easy to find. As one scene member, known only as "Ipggi," states, "The Internet made everything that was once so hard to obtain so easy. IRC, email, ftp and webpages all open to Joe public. And in 1994 they flooded in, drove after drove causing great despair among the many old schoolers."[21] The search for the computer underground was fueled by a decade of sensationalistic news reporting, which increasingly portrayed criminal hackers as powerful heroes or cowboys on the electronic frontier. Two more movies describing the computer underground were released in 1995, *The Net* and *Hackers,* both of which featured hackers as protagonists, further propagating an image of the all-powerful, renegade teenage hacker. While participants in the computer underground saw hackers and pirates as two different groups, the mainstream media did not. A decade later, a new generation of teenagers was introduced to a newly accessible Internet; they were all in search of the shadowy, powerful computer underground that they had heard so much about, and because warez trading took significantly less technical skill than actual hacking, many of them entered into the warez scene. As many of these new users were accessing the Internet through networks such as AOL and CompuServe—which offered their own private content, chat rooms, messaging, and file transfer tools—additional warez groups began to form inside these services, generally isolated from the BBS and

Internet scenes. Most notably, the AOL warez scene grew the fastest due to flaws in AOL software that allowed hacking programs, such as AOHell, to automate many warez group functions. Because AOL had a growing reputation for providing Internet access to a technically inept group, the AOL warez scene was looked down on by both the BBS software pirates and the Internet software pirates, who frequently referred to the AOL pirates as "lamerz."

As the warez scene flourished on the newly popularized Internet, the older pirate boards continued to decline. Law enforcement officials continued to bust underground boards and sysops through the 1990s, as they became increasingly familiar with computer technologies. Paranoia and fear spread among the BBS underground, as anyone could become an informant, and any board could become a sting operation. Additionally, the Business Software Alliance and the Software Publishers Association (SPA)—industry lobbyist groups formed by software developers—began to target sysops of pirate boards with civil lawsuits. In 1996, Microsoft and Novell settled a civil copyright case with the sysop of the Assassin's Guild BBS for over $70,000.[22] However, the new forms of Internet piracy did not go unnoticed by the groups, and later in the same year, the very first civil lawsuit for sharing files over the Internet took place between the SPA and Internet user Max Butler, who was making pirated software publicly available through an FTP server.[23] Many sysops simply shut down their boards, and hackers, phreaks, and warez groups began to leave the scene out of fear that they would be caught next. Until this time, law enforcement officers had focused primarily on hacking boards as they lacked the necessary legal tools to prosecute copyright infringement as a criminal offense. However, in 1997, the U.S. Congress passed amendments to copyright law, allowing for the criminal prosecution of nonprofit copyright violations. While largely ineffective, the changes allowed the Federal Bureau of Investigation to organize a crackdown specifically targeting pirate boards known as Cyberstrike.[24] Of those remaining, five of the more significant boards were seized, signaling to many BBS users the end of the pirate BBS scene.[25] But just as the BBS scene was beginning to die out, the unintended consequences of yet another new technology were beginning to become apparent online.

The Moving Pictures Experts Group had organized to establish new international standards for audio and video compression and created an International Standards Organization standard for audio compression in 1992 known as MPEG Layer 3. In 1995, the Fraunhofer Society publicly released the first MPEG Layer 3 audio compression software, coining the term *MP3*.[26] The software, which quickly inspired other free software implementations of MP3 compression, such as Nullsoft Winamp, allowed users to compress the relatively large WAV files found on CDs into much smaller MP3 files without a significant reduction in sound quality. At the time, compressing and decompressing (listening to) audio in MP3 format took a significant amount of processing power and storage space. However, as the average, entry-level personal computer became capable of creating and playing MP3 audio files, the format quickly became popular as a means to store and share digital audio. Warez groups devoted to releasing popular music albums in MP3 format appeared, and IRC rooms and FTP sites began to fill with music. As the cost of hard drive storage space fell, maintaining a digital audio library became increasingly feasible, particularly for those users technologically savvy enough to navigate the underground IRC channels. However, the popularization of MP3 audio provided the average Internet user (with available Web space) the necessary tools to share music as well. Combined with the online publishing capabilities of the World Wide Web, the MP3 allowed users to upload their music collections into public Web space, allowing anyone to access them. One demographic in particular had all of the necessary resources to share music via the Web: college students. In response to huge job growth in the technology sector, college campuses were establishing high-bandwidth networks and Internet connections to offer to incoming students, along with programs in information technology and computer science. Seeing the opportunity to share music with their peers, technologically savvy college students began using university networks to share MP3 files between computers. By 1996, the RIAA had identified this form of file sharing as a threat to their copyrights—three years prior to the development of Napster. At first, the RIAA contacted the operators of the Internet music archive sites available through the Web. After a period of 18 months, the RIAA then began filing civil lawsuits against those sites that had not responded to their warnings.[27]

This situation provided a fertile environment for the development of P2P file sharing: personal computers with highly customizable and standardized architectures, expanding network access and bandwidth, a history of copying, cultural association with the wild frontier of the Internet underground, lower-cost digital storage, and more portable formats for media. It would have been surprising had no one stepped in to develop a system to efficiently make use of these conditions. In the middle of these lawsuits concerning early file sharing, Shaun Fanning had begun teaching himself to program on his own first computer. His passion for programming landed him an internship at his uncle's company, NetGames, where he worked alongside Carnegie Mellon computer science students. Possibly more important to his computer education, however, was his discovery of IRC and everything that came along with it. His IRC handle was, of course, "Napster." While there isn't any concrete evidence that Fanning had any involvement with the computer underground, he was a member of the computer security research group w00w00. Fanning eventually became a computer science student at Boston's Northeastern University and began developing his own software. On the basis of conversations about MP3s he had with his roommate, he began to develop the Napster software. Fanning was encouraged and helped by w00w00 members—most notably Jordan Ritter—who eventually took over development of the server end of the software (see Chapter 3 for more information on how Napster worked). Fanning eventually devoted so much time to the development of Napster that he made the decision to leave Northeastern University to continue his work full-time. As part of the beta-testing period, Fanning released the software to a group of 30 friends, asking them to keep it confidential. They all loved the software—so much so that they decided to distribute the software to others, regardless of Fanning's request. Soon, over 3,000 people had downloaded the client software and were actively sharing MP3 files. Recognizing the potential of Napster, Fanning's uncle started a company and began raising investment capital. He had managed to raise $2 million by October 1999, and Fanning moved to Silicon Valley with Ritter to continue Napster development. One year later, Napster had an estimated 32 million users and was growing at a rate of 1 million users per month, until the network was shut down in 2001.[28]

So then, if warez groups, college students, and Web publishers were already sharing music in MP3 format—and consequentially, being sued by the RIAA—in 1997, two years before Napster, what caused all of the uproar in 1999, after Napster's release? While the networking model Fanning developed to drive Napster was itself fairly innovative, the technical specifics of Napster were largely invisible to the average user. Overall, Fanning did two things to make digital file sharing the widespread phenomenon it is today: he made it easier, and he took digital copyright violation out of the hands of the warez groups. Throughout the history of online file sharing, as the barriers to network access have fallen, the number of users in search of the underground has increased—and the majority of these users ended up in the warez scene, as the least technically challenging of the underground groups. Despite the fact that network/Internet access became increasingly easier over the years, file sharing prior to Napster was still beyond the grasp of the average Internet user, and as such, file sharers and warez d00ds were a minority. By placing the ability to share files online into the hands of the average user, file sharing appeared as a substantially different activity from that in which the warez scene typically engaged. The mainstream media had covered pirate busts and the computer underground, providing the general public with a sense of the unlawfulness of digital copyright infringement. But someone using Napster didn't fit the criminal image created by the media; rather, he was just an average Internet user sharing a few songs between friends—and that couldn't be illegal, could it? With that sense of the relationship between online file sharing and copyright, combined with the easy-to-use Napster software, Napster use skyrocketed. With Napster, finally, one could be part of online piracy without seeking out the computer underground and participating in the somewhat daunting and competitive warez scene. Additionally, computer processing power made MP3 encoding and decoding simple, and Internet service providers were beginning to offer high-bandwidth access through cable and digital subscriber lines (DSL). It became fast, easy, and cheap to download and store a massive digital music library. The last of the technical barriers to online file sharing had fallen, and it seemed that everyone was sharing something. As Julian Dibbell notes in an article chronicling his entry into music sharing, "For these are the times that try intellectual-property holders' souls, when music flies from hard drive to hard drive on wings of desire and in the face of every known law of copyright."[29]

Relatively fast processing power, cheap hard drive storage, high-bandwidth access to a global network designed for information sharing, a sense that sharing with friends is the right thing to do, the fuzzy nature of digital copyright, the construction of the warez criminal—each of these factors, in addition to an infinite number of other people, experiences, and technologies spanning throughout history, shaped and was crystallized into Napster. It was a confluence of technologies, values, and people that created the trajectory that allowed for the development and widespread acceptance of Napster. Unfortunately for the users of the service, Napster was extremely short-lived. By March 2001, Napster was effectively crippled following a court decision (discussed in Chapter 7). It was the same architecture that allowed users to quickly search for music made available by others that also provided the RIAA with a central point of attack. However, the concept represented by Napster—of allowing users to connect with each other, rather than to a single server spread—and new P2P networks with different architectures were quickly developed to fill the void left by the fall of Napster. In the next chapter, I'll describe how these P2P networks work and how Napster's architecture itself led to its downfall.

Chapter 3

P2P TECHNOLOGIES
AND THE WAREZ SCENE

Napster, and the technical architecture that supported it, was only the beginning of P2P file sharing's rise to popularity. But the architecture that Fanning developed was not *truly* P2P, and it was precisely because the Napster architecture was not true P2P that the network was shut down only a few years after it got started. Understanding the architecture that Fanning developed, and the changes made to that architecture by the software developers who followed, is critical to understanding how file sharing works, the risks file sharers take, and the legal challenges faced by copyright holders who have filed suits against file sharers and file-sharing networks. Unfortunately, not everyone actually knows enough about the ways in which computers and the Internet work together to allow for the creation and operation of P2P networks. Even those who have years of experience with computers and the Internet may have had no reason to actually open up the black box and try to figure out how everything fits together. Admittedly, it is a complex system—people in the field of information technology (IT) go to college for a reason. For now, you need to know enough about how computers and the Internet work before we can start looking at how the P2P systems that are layered on top of them work. In this chapter, we'll be starting out with a crash course in TCP/IP, the complex set of rules that govern how communication happens between computers online. If you're something of a technophobe, it is hoped that this crash course will not only prepare you to get a sense of how P2P works, but will also give you a little knowledge to impress your IT friends.

TCP/IP CRASH COURSE

Everyone talks about networks quite a bit, especially with all of the various mobile devices and tools available on the market today, but what *is* a network? Broadly defined, a network is simply a system of interconnected people and technologies across which information may be communicated. To communicate information of any kind, there needs to first exist an agreed on standard between the parties involved. Although you may not immediately recognize it as such, reading this book right now is an example: you, as the reader, and I, as the author, are relying on a shared understanding of a specific system of symbols—written English—to communicate. At the lowest level, computers use a binary system of symbols (1 and 0), but an agreed on system alone is not enough to allow communication to take place; there also needs to be some kind of method for transmitting information between parties, itself representing another system of agreed on rules for getting information from one place to another. Take the postal system, for example. When you want to send a letter to someone else, you don't simply write the letter and toss it into the mailbox, expecting the Post Office to sort it out. Instead, you put the letter into an envelope with a name and location written on it in a very specific format: an address. That address is then used by the Post Office to send your letter from one point to another in the postal network, using the best means available. While you don't generally see the process happening, and it happens exponentially more quickly than sending a letter, the methods that computers use to communicate over networks are similar in many ways to the postal mail system.

Despite the long and technical-sounding acronym, Transmission Control Protocol/Internet Protocol (TCP/IP) is just a set of rules that govern how computers communicate with each other over networks. There is no one thing called the Internet out there somewhere, no giant box that all the computers of the world connect to somehow, allowing them all to talk to one another. What we know as the Internet is really just the set of computers in the world that can communicate with each other using the rules provided by TCP/IP, and that are connected together by various wired and wireless infrastructure technologies. It is an *inter*connected system of *net*works, but unlike the postal system, each of those interconnected networks may be owned and operated by different people and organizations. Because all the people who own and operate the millions of different segments that make up the Internet follow the same rules—TCP/IP—every computer connected to the Internet can communicate with every other connected computer. Overall, TCP/IP can get a little technical and complex—and this is, after all, a book on file sharing, not networking. To keep things simple, let's use a Post Office analogy and pretend that your computer is like a house, and all of the programs running on your computer are the people living inside. The analogy can only be stretched so far, but it should work for our purposes.

When your computer is connected to the Internet, it is given what is known as an Internet protocol, or IP, address. IP addresses are usually[1] given to computers through an Internet service provider (ISP), such as Time Warner, Verizon, or AT&T, or by an organization that has high-bandwidth service through an ISP. These numbers act similarly to a street address but can change every time a computer reconnects to the Internet and are not necessarily associated permanently with one specific computer. That's all connecting to the Internet (or a computer network) really is—just receiving an address and allowing the computer to communicate with the other computers connected to the Internet. When a program needs to connect to another computer on the Internet for any reason, whether to open a Web page or to send a file, it first needs to establish a connection with the other computer. The computer user provides an address to the program in some way, whether it be a Web address (URL), an e-mail address, or the IP address of the computer itself, but an address that in some way can be translated back into an IP address. Using this address, the program sends a message to the remote computer that it wishes to establish a connection and waits for a reply. The address is used by machines known as routers, which connect multiple networks of computers together, to determine how to best send the message to its destination. When that reply is received, the computers begin transmitting information between each other. This information is typically spread between many envelopes, known as packets, each addressed specifically to a particular program running on a particular computer. These packets are then reassembled by the receiving computer, and the data are passed on to the correct program.

All communication on the Internet happens in this manner. There is no difference between Web surfing, video downloads, e-mail, instant messaging, or playing games online. It's all accomplished by different messages sent in the TCP/IP envelopes known as packets. Thinking again back to the mail system analogy, the postal system can be used for a variety of purposes. You can send postcards, letters, pictures, and packages, but regardless of content, anything that is sent through the postal system follows the same set of rules to get from sender to destination. Just as anyone can send any kind of mail to anyone else, performing many of the more specialized tasks that you see every day does not require some kind of special computer; rather, as a computer connected to the Internet, today your computer could become a Web server, an e-mail server, or a video game server, if it was running the right software. This flexibility is one of the major strengths of the TCP/IP system. Because any kind of content can be placed inside of TCP/IP packets, it is possible to layer other types of rule sets for communication on top of TCP/IP, essentially allowing there to be networks within networks. Going back to the postal analogy, imagine that you're the only one in your house who can read and write in Esperanto. Because you can read and write in Esperanto, you can send and receive letters from other people who can read and write Esperanto, which you send and receive in postal envelopes. This makes you part of the network of people who can read and write letters in Esperanto, which is dependent on you being part of the postal network. As the people living in your computer house, certain programs allow your computer to become a part of specific networks that are layered on top of TCP/IP such as those that understand the data transmitted by instant messaging programs or FTP software.

But as we talked about in the last chapter, personal computers were not always powerful enough to run the software to effectively perform many types of network tasks. Prior to the development of affordable personal computers, processing power, memory, and hard drive space were so expensive that many organizations could only afford one large, centralized computer. Returning again to the postal analogy, only the most expensive computer houses had enough space to allow more than a few program people to live inside. To share the resources that these mainframe computers provided, many dumb local terminals were connected to the mainframe, essentially acting as many monitors and keyboards that allowed many people to use the computer at once. The mainframe computer itself became known as a server because it provided services to the many terminals connected to it. The terminals that connected to the server to make use of those services were known as clients. In this way, organizations could save money by buying only one large and expensive server, which could be shared simultaneously by many other people through the network. This particular method of network computing, where many terminals connected into a more powerful, centralized computer to share resources, became known as the client-server model (see Figure 3.1).

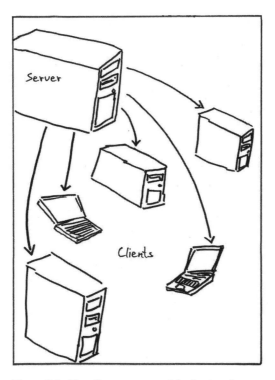

Figure 3.1. The client-server model of network computing.

For decades, the client-server model was the traditional method of doing (nearly) everything online. But as personal computers became increasingly powerful and inexpensive, the potential for each individual computer connected to the Internet to act as a server itself increased. Despite the increase in personal computing power, the client-server model prevailed throughout the file-sharing world into the late 1990s. Until that point, files were distributed by uploading them into a central location such as a bulletin board system (BBS), FTP site, or IRC host. While this method worked, the centralized server could only handle so many simultaneous connections. Imagine one program on a computer opening a connection with one other computer and keeping track of the communications between the two. Now, multiply that connection by 10, then by 100, or by 1,000—all connections that a single computer must manage and keep track of, using the limited amount of resources available to it. Large numbers of users could easily create the equivalent of an Internet traffic jam, overloading a single server into uselessness. Bandwidth is extremely expensive—many ISPs limit the amount of data that can be uploaded or downloaded to any given connection, and when that limit is passed, the charges increase. By comparison, the amount of resources required to download files from the server was extremely low. Difficulties such as these played a significant role in keeping the warez scene underground and away from the larger population of Internet users. Many release groups relied on compromised (hacked) computers to host pirated materials, rather than paying for the bandwidth themselves. Using centralized servers to host files solved another problem for warez traders: locating files. There simply was no easy way to search for files across multiple sites, so by uploading all of their files to one server, people looking for a particular file knew where to look because there were only a few servers to go to. This also kept the warez scene from the public eye because if everyone knew the location of a single server, that server would then become an easy target for law enforcement; therefore the locations of warez servers needed to be kept secret. Indeed, file sharing was only just barely sharing as we know it today. Very few people were actually sharing files for others to download, in comparison to the number of people who merely leeched files from sites, downloading files without giving anything back to the file-sharing community.

P2P file-sharing networks, as popularized by Napster, would radically change all the various practices and limitations that Internet users had come to accept when distributing large files across the Internet. In the client-server model, the server is required to expend the majority of the resources required to transfer a file, both in terms of network bandwidth and processing power. But developers of P2P networks began to realize that the computers acting as clients—the ones downloading the files—had access to bandwidth and processing power themselves. Personal computers on the Internet could *become* servers at the same time they acted as clients, simultaneously downloading and uploading files between each other, rather than relying on one centralized computer. Each computer in the network was equal to every other computer in the network and was referred to simply as a node, rather than as a client or a server. The P2P network model saved bandwidth and avoided the common traffic jams. Rather than forcing a small number of servers with limited bandwidth and processing power to expend the majority of resources required to distribute files, the cost was decentralized across all the nodes currently connected to the network. Those who wished to make a file available for distribution no longer needed to find a server and upload the file; rather, it could simply be hosted from the computer it was already on, just so long as that computer was connected to the Internet. P2P models harness the collective resources of a group of networked computers, allowing files to be distributed in more efficient ways.

Furthermore, the centralized servers (which made such attractive targets for law enforcement officials) could be eliminated. By making every node in the network a server, spreading the files to be shared across thousands of computers, it became much more difficult to shut down a file-sharing operation by disabling just one. The fact that the files available to the network were shared across many nodes, thereby reducing the number of files that any one node made available at a given time, effectively forced copyright holders to change their tactics in their battle to protect their rights—a topic we'll discuss in more detail in Chapter 7.

Because files are distributed across each node, all P2P file-sharing networks have two major problems to overcome: knowing which computers (addresses) are active nodes in the network and knowing which node has what files available. While the problem may appear simple at first glance, developing software that can search through the content of thousands of nodes (which may drop in and out of the network at any time) is extremely difficult. As such, different developers have approached the problem in different ways, resulting in many different networks with different characteristics. As such, not all P2P networks are completely decentralized. There are two classifications of P2P networks, hybrid P2P and true P2P, based on the level of centralization in the network. Each of the two types of network has particular strengths and weaknesses. However, keep in mind that there is a very large difference between a file-sharing *network* and the *software* that allows a computer to connect to that network. All P2P networks, whether they are hybrid or true P2P networks, are really just a group of computers that communicate with one another in a specific way. For each P2P network, there exists a number of client programs—the program people who can speak the P2P languages—that allow computers to connect into that network. Many P2P users often confuse the client they use to connect to a P2P network with the network itself. Further adding to the confusion, many developers of P2P networks also develop client software and give it the same name as the network itself—as in the cases of BitTorrent and Gnutella. While these clients all operate the same at the level of the P2P network itself, many offer various features and added functionality that can make P2P use easier and potentially safer.

Hybrid P2P

As the name implies, networks that utilize the hybrid P2P model still rely on the traditional client-server model to a certain extent. While files are still transferred directly between users in hybrid P2P networks, they rely on one or more centralized servers to perform a variety of different tasks. While these servers never actively store or share files on the network, they do send and receive types of information that allow the network to run, providing a *service* to all the nodes in the network. Because these servers play such a crucial role, and differ in function from all other nodes in the network, these types of network cannot be considered true P2P.

Strengths of Hybrid Systems

- Centralized management
- Fast, reliable searching

Weaknesses of Hybrid Systems

- Central point of failure

The most common function of a centralized server in hybrid P2P models is to act as a database of all files available on each node, essentially becoming an information center for any node searching for a particular file. As each node connects to the network, it sends a list of all the files shared by that node to the server. By combining all of the information about which node is sharing what file into one place, searching for files is extremely fast. When users of hybrid P2P networks search for a file, the client software contacts the central indexing server, which then responds with a list of all file names that match the search terms sent by the user. The search results contain information about which node is sharing the file, so when the user chooses a file to download from the search results, the node requesting the file establishes a direct connection with the node sharing the file. Implementing a file search system in this way serves a dual purpose. In addition to providing fast and reliable access to search results, a centralized server allows for an easy way for computers to connect to the network. The server essentially acts as a membership list, allowing any computer to know which other computers are connected to the network. Because the server is always in the same place online, using the same IP address, peers connecting to the network only need to know how to contact the server. Once connected, the server lets the peer know where to find all the other peers in the network (see Figure 3.2).

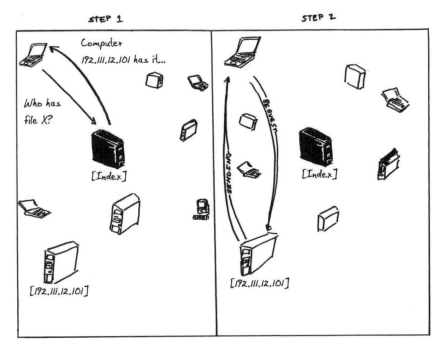

Figure 3.2. A hybrid P2P network.

While this type of architecture certainly solves the problems of determining which computers are part of the network and which nodes have what files, it has one potentially fatal flaw: if the central servers that manage network membership and file indexing go down, the entire network goes down. Without those central servers, no computer connecting to the network can contact any other, and hence, there is no network. This flaw was leveraged by members of the Recording Industry Association of America (RIAA) to successfully attack Napster and Aimster/Madster. By suing the businesses that administered the two networks (the reasons for the lawsuits will be discussed in Chapter 7), the RIAA shut down the servers that allowed the networks to run. This incentivized the development of P2P networks that were more decentralized and had no administrative organization to shut down. Simply because of the popularity of Napster, other developers had already begun work on other types of P2P networks in an effort to capitalize on such a large user base. Soon after the lawsuits against Napster and Aimster/Madster, these newer, more decentralized forms of P2P network—now known as pure or true P2P—became increasingly popular through the early 2000s, as hybrid P2P networks began to close their doors.

Common Examples of Hybrid Networks

- Napster (network)
  - Napster
  - Napigator
  - OpenNap

- DirectConnect (network)
  - DC++
  - Direct Connect
  - LinuxDC++

True P2P

From a computer science perspective, true P2P networks do not rely on centralized servers of any kind. All peers are equal in the network and may act as both client and server at any time. Completely pure P2P networks are very rare and extremely difficult to implement. The majority of true P2P networks still rely on servers, or supernodes, that have been given special responsibilities in the network, but to a much lesser extent than those typically utilized in hybrid P2P networks. Additionally, the more centralized nodes on which true P2P networks rely tend to be somewhat distributed themselves, and anyone can operate or act as one of these more centralized nodes (see Figure 3.3).

Strengths of True P2P Systems

- No central point of failure
- Increased (but not total) anonymity

Weaknesses of True P2P Systems

- Slow, unreliable search
- Network use relies on other users

The main benefit to this type of model is the lack of any centralized point of failure. Unlike in the hybrid model, the loss of any one peer from the network will not result in the shutdown of the entire network. This makes true P2P networks extremely resilient to attacks as there is no one specific target that will allow for damage to the network itself. However, because there is no server providing indexing and location services, many

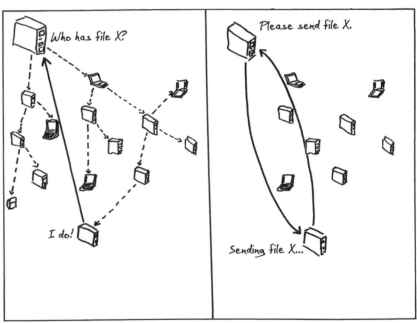

Figure 3.3. A true P2P network.

simple operations become extremely difficult. One of the major challenges faced by developers of true P2P systems is determining a method for a user to connect to the network at all. Imagine again that you can read and write in Esperanto, and you want to send letters to others who can do the same. Obviously, there are other people out there who can read and write in Esperanto, but you need their addresses to send them letters and connect to the Esperanto letter network. How would you find out who these people are and where they live?

Computers connecting to a true P2P network have a similar problem. To connect to become part of the network, there needs to be some way to know which other computers are already connected. To solve this problem, some networks (such as Gnutella) require first-time users to find lists of known IP addresses, which provide the addresses of other users who are known to be using the network at the time the list was created. These lists can frequently be found on various Web sites devoted to hosting these lists. Once the first-time user has found and connected to another computer in the network, she receives a new list of known addresses from that computer. Searching for files is also a challenge as there exists no central repository of shared files.

In the majority of true P2P networks, searches for files are spread through-out the network. When a node searches for a particular file, the search terms are sent from the original computer to all other known nodes. Those nodes that receive the search term then search through the files they are sharing, return the search results (if any) to the node that requested the search, then pass the search term on to the nodes of which it is aware. In this way, search terms are spread throughout the network, peer by peer, and search results are slowly sent in to the original searcher. Unlike with the search method used by hybrid P2P networks, the entire network is not always searchable, particularly as the number of participating nodes increases. To limit the amount of resources used by any one search, a search request is given a time to live, or TTL. The TTL specifies how many times a search request should be passed on to other nodes. Because there is a limit on how many times requests are passed on, the entire network is not polled for any given search term; therefore, if only one node in the network has the file you're looking for, you may not be able to find it. Not being able to find all of the available files in a network is something of a double-edged sword, though. By slightly segmenting the network in this way, those attempting to identify nodes sharing specific (usually copyrighted) files are less likely to find all the nodes sharing those files, effectively providing a very thin additional layer of anonymity to true P2P network users.

With true P2P networks, there are few targets available to copyright holders that would allow them to cease the operation of any given network, as there were with Napster and Aimster/Madster. Some true P2P networks, such as KaZaA and Grokster, were shut down through legal action, but this was due to the fact that the businesses that maintained the client were sued. There are always individual users, however. As file sharers began to move toward the more decentralized, true P2P networks, the RIAA and the Motion Picture Association of America began to take legal action against individu-als using P2P networks to share copyrighted works. As we'll discuss in the coming chapters, this has not proven to be a particularly effective strategy overall, but individual civil suits from the intellectual property industry remain a threat for all P2P users who share copyrighted materials.

Common Examples of True P2P Networks

- Gnutella (network)
  - LimeWire
  - BearShare

- FastTrack (network)
  - Grokster
  - KaZaA
  - iMesh
- AresP2P (network)
  - AresP2P
- eDonkey2000 (network)
  - eDonkey2000
  - eMule/eMule Plus
  - Shareaza

BitTorrent

One commonly used form of P2P network stands apart from all the others: BitTorrent. While it can technically be categorized as a true P2P network, the ways in which BitTorrent operates sets it apart from all the other networks currently in popular use. Developed by Bram Cohen in 2001, the BitTorrent network takes the concept of P2P file sharing one step further. Rather than distributing multiple files across many peers and allowing them to connect directly to one another, BitTorrent distributes many parts of a single file across multiple users and then allows the users to send and receive those parts among each other until all of them have received all of the parts. This method distributes the bandwidth costs among all of the users who wish to receive the file, making it particularly useful for quickly distributing one file among many users. Because all available bandwidth is used across all of the computers in the network, it is possible to download files through BitTorrent extremely quickly. One server, known as a seeder, starts off with the file being shared in entirety and then distributes parts of that file to the clients, known as peers or leechers, who distribute the parts among themselves. As peers complete their downloads, they become seeders themselves, further distributing parts of the file to those who still require it. By allowing peers to download parts of the file from other peers, a situation in which many peers are attempting to download a file simultaneously is desirable. As more peers attempt to download the file, the pieces of the file can be distributed more quickly. The group of computers engaged in downloading any given file, or set of files, is known as a swarm (or occasionally, a cloud; see Figure 3.4).

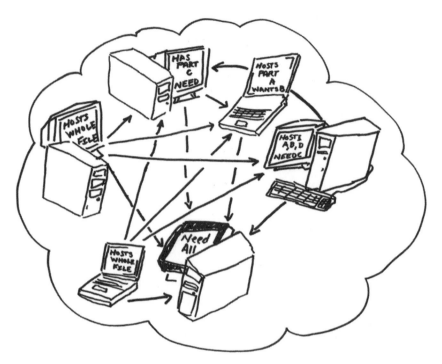

Figure 3.4. A BitTorrent swarm.

Strengths of BitTorrent

- Potential for very fast file transfer
- Large numbers of downloaders increases download speed (to a point)
- No potential for accidental sharing of files

Weaknesses of BitTorrent

- Semicentralized trackers and torrent sites
- Transfer is slow with few peers/seeders
- Participation in BitTorrent networks requires simultaneous uploading and downloading
- Leech problems can arise when downloaders leave the swarm without seeding

While high volumes of traffic are actually beneficial for BitTorrent swarms, BitTorrent has no built-in search capabilities, and there is no broader network per se. Users connect to a somewhat isolated network—a swarm, consisting only of those who are downloading the same file or set of files.

To connect to the swarm distributing any given file (or set of files), a user must first locate the torrent file for that swarm, which contains information known as metadata, used by BitTorrent clients to determine tracker location and file size, among other things. Specific Web sites are devoted to hosting millions of torrent files, holding the keys to torrent swarms of all types of content. These torrent sites act in place of a centralized server, allowing users to search for specific files. Because torrent sites are not actively part of a BitTorrent network, they are not considered when categorizing the network as hybrid P2P or true P2P. Additionally, BitTorrent relies on a specialized server, known as a tracker, that tracks which peers have which parts of the file being distributed. The tracker manages connections between peers, determining the best possible method for the file to be distributed across the group of seeders and peers. While the tracker typically performs this job, the BitTorrent protocol has increasingly added support for swarms that do not rely on trackers to transfer files, allowing transfers to continue even if the tracker is not currently online.

Common Examples of BitTorrent Clients

- uTorrent
- Azureus
- BitComet
- BitTorrent
- BitTornado

WHERE DO P2P FILES COME FROM?

File-sharing networks have made it extremely easy and fast to share and copy digital files of any kind. Obviously, people frequently share the files they have themselves, whether they were created or copied by the person sharing them or downloaded from another file sharer. Either way, the files have to come from *somewhere*. It just so happens that the software that allows you to access those files makes it somewhat easy to forget that somebody somewhere has to do quite a bit of work to make the files you download and share, as those who have actually had to rip a DVD or album know. Just think of all the effort that must have gone into all those files, each user ripping and encoding and compressing his movies, music, and software. Well, as it turns out, that doesn't really happen so much. The masses didn't come to P2P networks because they were a hassle to use; rather, they came to P2P networks because the networks are *convenient*.

While it is technically possible that all the files available on file-sharing networks come from individual file sharers, who are simply sharing the music, movies, and software they personally purchased, that is not exactly the way things always work on file-sharing networks—it just doesn't make sense. If the majority of people sharing files on P2P networks are too lazy to actually encode the content properly, where do all these files come from? Well, some of them do come from ambitious P2P users who just want to share. If you think back to Chapter 2, we briefly talked about the warez scene as part of the computer underground through the 1980s and 1990s: these groups were primarily responsible for obtaining, cracking, managing, and making available the majority of pirated digital material during their time. Well, despite the federal crackdown that happened during that period, the international warez scene is still thriving today, and a large percentage of the files available on P2P networks are the result of the warez groups doing what they do best: ripping, cracking, encoding, and releasing.

The warez scene can seem more than a little strange to an outsider—thousands of skilled IT users, all racing to get the highest-quality content they can find released onto the Internet before any of it is available for sale, all without any financial benefit and frequently at risk of federal prosecution. To the people who compose the warez scene, however, it's all a big game. The reward is prestige and respect among the other scene members, in addition to increasingly higher levels of access to pirated content. You may be wondering at this point, "That's it? They actually risk jail time just to move some software or movies around? Really?" Well, yes. For the people involved, it is truly a sport, requiring (in some cases) skill, intelligence, and perseverance. Besides, a truly epic *scene release* can make world headlines. One example of this was the release of Star Wars movies onto P2P networks prior to their release in theaters. How does all of that happen? Who finds this content before it comes to store shelves or movie screens? How does a CD or DVD become a scene release?

Overall, the entire process is more difficult than you might think. While some of those in the warez scene prefer to work alone, the majority work in groups, dividing the various tasks among themselves. Finding the content, breaking the (increasingly common) copyright protection, properly encoding the content into the correct file format, compressing the file for efficient transfer, and finally, moving files between the top pirate servers and boards for the pre- and official release are all separate tasks requiring specific technical skill sets, representing different positions in the warez group hierarchy.

COMMENTS ON THE SCENE FROM THE PIRATE BAY

tw*** at 2008–09–19 23:27 CET:

Just want to ask a quick question here because I'm curious and don't get it. Why are so many people so eager to rip and download screen caps of movies? What is the urgency that you can't wait for a decent DVDrip to come out? Surely when a good clean copy comes out you replace the poor copies and I just don't get why anyone bothers with questionable copies at all. Perhaps someone here can explain.

Also just want to add a massive and great thanks to all the wonderful posters and seeders of brilliant DVDrips without whom my little movie collection (which I love) would not exist.

----

vista******* at 2008–09–20 02:46 CET:

The rush is out because that's how the pirate scene works.

Take a look at bi****** [another uploader] profile of uploads, he does an outstanding job. Getting DVD screeners is a pump. Means you got the inside sources. Means you get into other areas that are not on torrents.

This process has remained somewhat unchanged through the decades following the BBS pirate scene, with the notable exception of additional roles as the types of digital content made available through pirate networks increased. Different groups typically focus on different types of content, each of which requires a varying level of effort to prepare and release.

It all starts with someone, somewhere, who is willing to obtain and share a copy of the content with the release group. This person is known as the supplier. Whether it be a music album, a movie, software, a book, or images (among other things), the hard part is finding a copy before it is officially released to the public. The fastest way to gain respect in the warez scene is to obtain, prepare, and release digital content onto the Internet, preferably before it is officially released to the public. For example, finding and releasing a copy of the highly anticipated video game Duke Nukem Forever (which has been in development for over 12 years and has yet to officially hit store shelves) would immediately gain a would-be pirate hero status in the warez scene, in addition to making headlines across the Internet. Of course, as a yet unfinished and unreleased game, Duke Nukem Forever is likely protected by intense physical and network security, so actually managing to obtain a copy would be incredibly difficult and time consuming for most people. The easiest method of obtaining content before its release is to work for the company that produces it and somehow steal a copy from the job site. Finding someone willing to risk her job to gain respect in the warez scene is fairly difficult to do, so groups often have to find other means to obtain the content. The methods vary, but members of the warez scene have been known to hack into corporate networks, purchase copies released in other countries, and obtain access to review copies of content. Not all content can be obtained prior to release, so occasionally, pirate groups simply buy the content off store shelves or record it using a camcorder in a movie theater.

Once the content is obtained by the supplier, the group then begins preparing it for release. Frequently, the first step in this process is to remove any copyright protection from the content. As early as the 1980s, software developers were aware that their software was being copied and shared by computer users, so they began devising methods to ensure that copying became as difficult as possible. If you have ever installed a piece of

FROM AN INTERVIEW WITH A WAREZ SCENE MEMBER

NF: Tell me a little bit about what an average day in the scene was like for you.

M: Basically I would wake up and hang out in an IRC channel when I was free. The couriers had more day-to-day work. Suppliers and crackers also did a good bit of work.

For a short while I worked as a supplier, someone would pay for a game to be delivered to me on its release day. It would be express shipped to me, and I would have contacted the parcel service in order to get the shipment as quickly as possible. In the scene speed was, and still is key, the first group to release a working copy of the goods won. It was my job to upload a copy of the game as fast as possible to our group distribution site. After that had been done, it was up to our cracking team to create whatever cracks were required. After the cracks were created it was my job to package the release and upload it to our primary distribution servers.

expensive software yourself, you may have been required to enter a lengthy license code—this is one example of copyright protection. That code is unique and may only be used once to activate the software, preventing further copies from being installed on other computers with the same code. As the years passed, this created something of a competition between the software developers and the crackers devoted to breaking the protections that were built into the software. Now, there are copyright protections on nearly every form of media, including software, console games, movies, and music. Unfortunately for the copyright holders, these forms of protection tend to be broken quickly by the crackers racing to make the content available to the warez scene, but they do make it difficult for less technical users to casually make copies for friends and family. The process of cracking copyright protections from software ranges in difficulty, depending on the mechanisms used to secure the content, but usually requires a high level of technical skill. Once the copyright protection is removed from the content, fully operational copies may created and distributed.

In the case of releases containing music or movies, the next person to receive the content is known as the encoder. Raw digital audio and video files are extremely large—too large, in fact, to easily store or transmit across the Internet. The encoder determines the best way to reduce the file size of the content by encoding it into the appropriate file format. One of the most simple examples of this is the conversion of raw audio files from CDs into the MP3 format. Encoding video files, however, is much more complex: encoders must decide between different file containers, which hold different types of encoded audio, video, and subtitle formats, and then choose the type of encoding that will best fit the audio and video content of the release. The process of encoding is a trade-off between three factors: the size of the file, the quality of the image/audio, and the computing resources needed to actually play the file without slowdown. The primary goal of the encoder is to significantly reduce the size of the content without a significant loss in quality, while still allowing the average computer to play the content. The role of the encoder has become increasingly important, as additional emphasis has been placed on higher and higher audio and video quality, elevating the job of encoding almost to an art. Encoders who reliably produce high-quality releases with significantly reduced file sizes quickly gain notoriety in the scene.[2]

All releases, whether or not they require encoding into a specific file format, must then be compressed prior to being officially released, which is typically done by the packager. The process of compression reduces the file size of a release even further than encoding does. After it has been compressed, the process of decompression is typically somewhat slow, and in the case of music and movie files, it is often too slow to allow the file to be played at the same time it is being decompressed.[3] Even those who are unfamiliar with P2P file transfer have likely come across compressed files at one time or another. The most commonly known compression format is the ZIP format. Although ZIP compression is only one of many digital compression formats, many improperly call digital compression "zipping" a file. Compression is critical for sharing files via file-sharing networks as the smaller a file is, the more quickly it can be transferred across the network. The compression process requires little skill and is often slow, tedious work. As such, packagers tend to be less highly regarded than the other operators in warez groups. Once the packager has completely compressed the file, and included some information about what is contained in the file and details about the release group in what is known as an NFO file, the content is ready for release.

Finally, the group courier receives the release and begins transferring it between the top-level sites (topsites), which supply the warez scene as a whole. These sites serve as storehouses for the scene and as such are capable of storing extremely large amounts of content—commonly multiple terabytes of space. Couriers are usually the least respected level of the warez scene, and many work independently of any group. To gain entry to both the topsites and group releases, they compete with one another to determine who can most quickly transfer files between servers. By moving the release between these servers, the release is communicated to all the other scene groups and members. Some topsites are run by specific groups, while others are independently run, very similar to the structure of the BBS scene in the 1980s and 1990s.

It is at this point, with the release distributed among the major topsites, that the majority of warez scene members would prefer the distribution ended. All the other groups are aware of, and can access, the release, and nobody else. Unfortunately, seeing the distribution chain end here is rarely, if ever, the case. Some members of the warez scene are also part of a secondary, more risky scene known as the FXP scene. FXP groups look for vulnerable computers connected to the Internet, break into them, and covertly convert them for use as *distros,* hacked servers used to further distribute warez releases outside of the warez scene network. Warez scene members tend to look down on FXP groups, whose participation in risky and highly visible operations can easily lead to capture by law enforcement. In comparison to the warez scene topsites, FXP distros are far less secure and can be easily accessed by those outside of the warez scene. As such, once a scene release is transferred to an FXP site, it is then quickly distributed on P2P networks by nonscene members with access to the distro. The entire process, from scene release to appearance on the P2P networks, can take as few as six hours, according to one FXP group member.[4] Of course, once a release hits the P2P networks, it spreads quickly— particularly if the content is popular.

So it all starts with someone with a (vaguely) legitimate copy, which is then cracked, ripped, compressed, and distributed all across the Internet. Of course, not all releases happen exactly like this; rather, some members of the warez scene work independently, some pirate groups operate entirely through P2P networks, and some P2P users just share what they have outside of any scene altogether. It all has to come from somewhere, however, and the amount of effort that goes into any given file available on P2P networks should not be taken for granted. Additionally, the files available on any given site or P2P network should never be attributed to the network, or the operators of the network, themselves. All the files come from people sharing with other people, and the network is simply a means of transport. After all that, there's a small possibility that you're interested in figuring out how to actually take advantage of these releases and get hooked into a P2P network for yourself.

USING P2P CLIENTS

No, I'm not really going to provide you with a detailed guide on how to use a P2P client. I'm not going to show you where to find them, how to install them, or how to configure them. I'm especially not going to show you how to go about finding illegitimately copied files to download. For one, I would prefer not to facilitate online piracy, regardless of my own personal beliefs about the ethicality of the illegal use of P2P. Besides, there are plenty of other books and guides out there available to anyone willing to do a quick Google search. Second, you don't need a guide—most of these programs are fairly self-explanatory. That said, for the uninitiated, downloading, installing, configuring, and using a P2P client may certainly seem to be a daunting task. Much to the dismay of the intellectual property industry, this could not be further from the truth. As we discussed in Chapter 2, one of the major reasons the use of P2P networks has become so popular is simply because they are extremely easy to use, even for those who are less experienced with computer technology. Indeed, to become and remain successful, P2P clients *must* be easy to use. Without a large user base, the network would be largely useless. To make sure that many people use your software (and share their files), anyone needs to be able to use it. The original Napster client interface was straightforward and intuitive—after all, the only difficult part was choosing which songs to search for. Most of the P2P clients that have followed after Napster have capitalized on the familiarity of the original Napster client and have adopted a similar interface.

As such, the majority of P2P client interfaces are composed almost entirely of a text box, which handles search terms; a window in which search results are displayed; and a window that provides status updates on files being transferred. Of course, many networks have additional features, such as chat rooms, node browsing, and media players, but for the most part, all of the major P2P clients will have a search bar, search results, and a transfer status indicator. The one major exception (as usual) is BitTorrent. Currently BitTorrent does not support any form of searching between swarms. The torrent sites are solely responsible for developing and maintaining search engines, and the interfaces between these sites may vary. Additionally, the client itself is composed almost exclusively of a transfer status window, simply displaying the status of any files currently being transferred.

Honestly, the best way to learn how to use P2P clients is simply to download one and get started. If you aren't sharing copyrighted files, your risk is fairly limited, so just go find something in the public domain (a legal distinction; see Chapter 7 for more information) and try to download it. Go find and download some of the larger open source software (e.g., OpenOffice.org, a *free* alternative to Microsoft Office) through a BitTorrent client. You'll learn far more than I could possibly explain to you here, and it is hoped that you'll end up with a useful piece of free software. If you choose not to use BitTorrent, search for something via the Gnutella network. However, for those of you looking to take the risk and download copyrighted works, be sure to read the next chapter first. We'll discuss all the risks of file sharing and how to avoid them. Regardless of what you choose to download, experiencing P2P networks for yourself is the best way to learn—not only will you end up with some useful (and, it is hoped, public domain) files, but you'll additionally get a sense for the differences between the networks, what types of files you can find, and possibly how to configure and uninstall P2P clients, when necessary. For more information, see Appendix B for links to P2P guides and support forums. As with nearly any technical endeavor, learning how to use online search engines for support can be one of your most important tools. Finally, if you are in any way afraid of using P2P networks—or computers and the Internet, for that matter—actively engaging with them is the best way to overcome those fears. That said, before jumping right in, take a look at the next chapter, where I'll discuss the risks that you do face as a P2P user. While that might sound a little foreboding, just remember that the risks are extremely small and manageable, especially if you choose to steer clear of copyrighted files—and you would never download or share a copyrighted file, right?

Chapter 4

MANAGING P2P RISK

Despite the fact that there are literally millions of other file sharers out there, uploading and downloading 24 hours a day, if you choose to join them, you, too, become a target. A variety of dangers are associated with P2P file sharing, and while the risk of encountering these dangers is somewhat small, the consequences are potentially very severe—particularly for those sharing copyrighted or illegal content. Those legally sharing files, without violating copyright laws, have much less to worry about, for somewhat obvious reasons. If you do decide either to download or upload files through P2P networks, this chapter discusses some of the dangers you could expect to encounter.

MALWARE

Currently it's fairly difficult to find someone who has never heard of a computer virus before. However, what fewer people know is that viruses represent only a segment of software developed to spread and do harmful things to your computer. As a whole, these forms of harmful software are referred to simply as malware (short for *malicious software*). This term was coined as an attempt to acknowledge the growing number of different types of harmful software, each developed to perform different malicious tasks. The term *computer virus* only refers to one increasingly rare type of malware, which requires human interaction to execute and spread. Computer viruses are one form of malware that can be spread through P2P networks, but the larger threat comes from newer forms, which are designed for more financially motivated tasks. The most common of these newer types of malware are spyware and adware, which surreptitiously monitor user activity and display unwanted advertisements, respectively. These forms of software are typically bundled together and provide the original developer with some form of financial reward, as marketing companies can use information to target advertisements, for which they then receive revenue. The more people running the adware and spyware, the more valuable the advertisement slots become. The legality of adware and spyware is somewhat unclear in many states, but there are other forms of malware, spread via P2P networks, that are more clearly fraudulent. Botnet clients, which allow infected computers to be remotely controlled and manipulated, can facilitate a wide range of fraudulent activities. By installing botnet clients on thousands of computers, botnet herders can relay spam e-mail, transfer files, and (most commonly) send immense amounts of traffic to a single Internet site, effectively shutting the target down. The newest form of malware to begin circulating is known as ransomware. This type of software encrypts files on a computer, making them unreadable, and demands that the computer user send money to the developer to decrypt the files, making them readable once again.

Malware represents a threat to P2P users in two separate ways. The first, and most obvious, threat comes from the potential to accidentally download malware or infected files from P2P networks. Because millions of people use them every day, P2P networks make an attractive target for those looking for ways to spread malicious software. This is typically done in either one of two ways: by simply renaming an infected file or malicious executable (program) or by infecting or including malware along with a legitimate file. The second method is much more difficult to detect than the first as the downloader actually receives the files he expected, unaware that his computer has been compromised. Both methods rely on downloaders choosing to search for and download the malicious files. As such, attackers choose file names that are most likely to draw in the most downloaders. These files typically make the malware appear as if it were pornography, a popular unreleased movie, or a popular game. Because this form of attack is both easy to execute and difficult to detect, it is used to distribute some of the more malicious malware such as viruses, botnet clients, and ransomware.

The second, somewhat less obvious vector for malware attack through P2P networks is through the P2P client software itself. Some software programs providing access to P2P networks are either themselves malware or come bundled with forms of malware. When the user downloads and installs the client, the malware is installed along with it. The most notorious of these was the KaZaA client, which had bundled both adware and spyware along with the client itself. Infected or bundled P2P client software is currently less of a threat than it was in the early 2000s, when many businesses were being formed around P2P networks and planned to profit off of advertising revenue generated by adware and spyware. Because this type of malware distribution can typically only be performed by the organization making the client available for download, and the motive for distributing the malware (usually spyware and adware) is monetary, the payloads associated with this type of distribution tend to be less destructive and malicious. However, there are still malicious P2P clients and malware-bundled P2P clients available for download today.

UNKNOWN/UNWANTED FILE CONTENTS

Simply put, it is impossible for someone to know the actual contents of a file until she has finished downloading it. This makes it difficult for someone downloading files via a P2P network to determine if the file contains malware, and it also makes it difficult to determine if the file actually contains the data the file name describes. This problem may not initially appear threatening; however, there exists the potential for accidental exposure to both regulated and illegal materials, a problem that becomes particularly salient given the ease by which minors may access pornographic content through P2P networks.

While the myth that the majority of Internet content is pornographic is largely false, with an estimated 1 percent of the Internet devoted to pornographic content,[1] even a small percentage of the Internet still represents an extremely large amount of content.P2P networks are no different, and the pornographic content available on these networks is highly popular. Through a study performed in 2006, the NPD group determined that 60 percent of the video content downloaded via P2P networks contained pornographic content.[2] This alone represents a problem for parents and adults, who must supervise minors who use P2P networks. Pornographic content is easily accessed through P2P networks and can be difficult to filter out of nonpornographic search results, making it difficult to prevent even unintentional exposure. Leveraging the popularity of common search terms, less reputable pornographic Web sites frequently name files containing advertisements for their services in misleading ways in an attempt to gain the widest possible audience for their commercials.

Minors are not the only ones at risk of being exposed to unwanted pornographic materials. Given the popularity of pornographic material, and the relative anonymity of P2P file sharing, P2P networks make attractive places to trade and share illegal child pornography. Additionally, file names can often be misleading, making it impossible to ensure that pornographic content downloaded through P2P networks depicts only subjects who are of legal age. Further complicating the issue, different countries have different legal definitions of child pornography, meaning that it may be legal for a P2P user in one country to share a pornographic file, but illegal for a P2P user in another country to download or store it. Concerns over potentially illegal pornographic materials available through P2P networks led the U.S. Government Accounting Office (GAO) to conduct a study in 2005. Using the three most popular P2P networks available at the time, the GAO conducted searches for both pornographic and nonpornographic keywords. On all the networks studied, searches using nonpornographic keywords targeting popular singers and cartoons resulted in at least some pornographic content. Additionally, when actively searching for pornographic content, results containing confirmed child pornography were found on two of the three networks.[3] While problems with accidental exposure to pornographic materials is an obvious problem, the far larger risk comes from accidental exposure to child pornography. The laws regarding child pornography are extremely strict, and once an individual is found in possession of pornographic content involving minors, it can be very difficult to explain that the acquisition of that content was accidental. As evidenced by the media coverage surrounding such cases, even those who are found not guilty may have difficulties with distancing themselves from the connection to child pornography.

SHARING SENSITIVE INFORMATION

The fact that many P2P clients publicly share files represents a significant risk to personal and organizational information security. Many users of file-sharing networks, such as Gnutella and KaZaA, accidentally share the contents of their entire computer when setting preferences in the client software. Typically included in these files are copyrighted files and sensitive personal information such as financial records and contact information. Because these types of files are typically named in similar ways, making them easy to find for the computer owners, attackers can easily search P2P networks to find and download this sensitive information. Depending on the amount of information made available by a single user, attackers may easily use that information for identity theft and other forms of fraud. Here again, P2P networks can create problems for parents supervising P2P use. Without an understanding of what is actually being stored on the computer, children can easily expose these forms of information to the public, without the knowledge of their parents. Under a Windows operating system, many P2P clients run in the background, visible only as an icon in the system tray. As the client runs, all the files set to be shared are available to the entire network.

Given the availability of computers and high-bandwidth Internet connections in current workplaces, many major organizations are particularly affected by this form of vulnerability, as their employees download and install P2P clients without thought as to which files are being shared. In cases such as these, far more than a single individual's personal information is at risk; trade secrets, personal information, and otherwise confidential information can be quickly and unknowingly leaked to the public. This, combined with the potential liability faced by organizations for copyright violations and bandwidth costs, has led most corporate and government organizations to ban P2P clients from their networks entirely. However, no organization stands alone, allowing consulting firms and contractors to act as unregulated access points into the confidential information of otherwise P2P-free organizations. An informal search by a security researcher at the University of Florida on the Gnutella network yielded credit card numbers, bank account information, confidential clothing designs, cellular tower maps, and the files of a government consulting firm. Searching through one Gnutella user's files, the researcher found a massive cache of personal information, containing dozens of credit reports and tax returns. He found another person searching for and downloading confidential information—someone who had herself forgotten to change the settings allowing people to search through what she had downloaded.[4]

Beyond problems caused when personal or sensitive information is accidentally shared via P2P networks, misconfiguration of P2P clients can potentially lead to more direct and visible consequences. The wide majority of computers store extremely large amounts of copyrighted files. Nearly every program, song, and movie stored on a computer—including the very files that compose the operating system itself (with the exception of computers running open source operating systems)—is a copyrighted work. Sharing those files, even unintentionally, is a violation of copyright. By doing so, even those who intended to use P2P networks for legal purposes may find themselves targeted by another type of danger faced by the majority of P2P users.

COPYRIGHT VIOLATION

While malware, unknown file contents, and accidental sharing of sensitive information are dangers that all P2P users face, there is an additional risk that those who share copyrighted files take: being found out by the copyright holders or those who have an interest in protecting copyright. When viewed through the lens of copyright law, P2P users are malicious attackers infringing on the copyrights of others, and the danger lies in the legal consequences of that infringement. For copyright industry insiders, sharing copyrighted works through P2P networks simply equates to theft (a position which is frequently debated), and anyone who engages in such practices should be treated as a thief. As such, copyright holders and service providers have gone to great lengths to fight P2P file sharing, in all its forms. While locating and suing P2P users has been the most publicized tactic used by intellectual property stakeholders, there are actually a wide variety of different practices used by these stakeholders to prevent the sharing of copyrighted works. All these methods can potentially affect P2P users in negative ways. It should be noted that most of these tactics have been used primarily by the recording industry, specifically the Recording Industry Association of America (RIAA), which has largely fought the hardest against copyright infringement over P2P networks. However, the majority of the tactics share one major goal, and one which fits with the strategies of all the major content producers: to make file sharing inconvenient for people who download and share copyrighted works.

The most dangerous (to P2P users) and widely publicized of these tactics is to monitor and locate P2P users who share copyrighted works. Nearly all major copyright holders, including record labels, movie studios, and software development firms, track and monitor online file sharing in different ways. The reasons for each of these organizations to do so vary, ranging from simple data collection to full civil litigation. We'll go into more detail on what happens when a P2P user is targeted by the intellectual property industry for further legal action in Chapter 7, but for now, let's take a look at how and why these copyright holders can identify and locate file sharers at a technical level. As we discussed previously, when a computer connects to the Internet, it is (typically) provided with an Internet protocol (IP) address by its Internet service provider (ISP) or managing organization. Connecting to other computers on P2P networks is no different than any other form of communication online, and as such, IP addresses are used to send and receive data between P2P nodes. These IP addresses are commonly tied to individual user accounts by ISPs. As such, IP addresses can be used to identify Internet users, but only if the ISP provides the information that ties an IP address (and the network traffic associated with that IP address) to a specific account. Despite the well-publicized threat of being identified while sharing copyrighted works via P2P networks, relatively little has been done to mask the IP addresses of P2P users, primarily due to the technical challenges involved. As such, obtaining the IP addresses of P2P users is a relatively trivial task. To retrieve the IP addresses of those sharing copyrighted works, one can simply connect to the network, search for a particular copyrighted file, and attempt to download the file. Because communicating with another computer in a P2P network requires both computers to know the IP address of the other—just as in our postal system example, to communicate, both parties must know the address of the other—by attempting to initiate a file transfer between the computer that is sharing the file and a computer controlled by an antipiracy group, the IP address of the computer sharing the file can be made available. This is often done through software that automates the process using a list of the titles of copyrighted works, created by copyright holders, as search terms. The modified P2P client software goes through the list, searching for matching files. When a match is found, steps are taken to verify that the file contents match the file name, an attempt is made to initiate communication with the computer sharing the file, and then the IP address of that computer is logged for future use. Currently this method only identifies users who make files available, or upload files, to other users. Users who only download copyrighted files, which is impossible on some P2P networks (such as BitTorrent), are safe from such methods—for the time being.

While identifying and threatening infringing P2P users is largely a means to emphasize the legal consequences of sharing copyrighted works, other tactics have been used by copyright holders to actively prevent P2P users from accessing copyrighted files. The most common method is to flood the P2P network with files that share the name of popular copyrighted works but do not actually contain the content described so that,

HOW THE RECORDING INDUSTRY ASSOCIATION OF AMERICA IDENTIFIES P2P USERS

Traditionally, the intellectual property industry is somewhat tight-lipped about the means by which they identify copyright-infringing P2P use. Providing too much detail about how P2P users can be identified could potentially allow someone to determine a method for circumventing the detection process. Additionally, those who publicly describe their personal connection to any means by which infringing P2P use is restricted or monitored tend to quickly gather large amounts of hate mail. However, the Recording Industry Association of America (RIAA) recently provided some detail about the method it uses to identify users of the Gnutella P2P network, known to many simply as LimeWire, in an article published by the *Chronicle of Higher Education*.[a] As an organization representing an association of different recording studios, one of the duties of the RIAA is to maintain a list of the works of which the members of the RIAA own the distribution rights. Obviously, this list is extremely large and contains the vast majority of available popular music. The RIAA then provides this list to a company known as MediaSentry (recently purchased by SafeNet), which specializes in covertly monitoring P2P networks. Using the list and proprietary software, MediaSentry connects to the network and searches for each song, gathering and recording search results. To other users on the network, MediaSentry simply looks like any other user searching for popular music, assuming they even notice that someone searched through their files at all. For each successful search result collected, the MediaSentry software then has the capability to browse all the files made available by the user sharing the song originally searched for and checks those file names against the RIAA list. While this would appear to be enough evidence, this only allows MediaSentry to know that a given user is sharing files that are *named* similarly to songs on the RIAA list. After all, anyone can name a file any way she chooses—it's what the file contains that really matters. So MediaSentry uses a variety of tactics to determine if a file actually contains one of the songs listed by the RIAA. First, for each file name that matches the list, the MediaSentry software attempts to use what is known as a hash value—which can potentially identify a unique file—to determine if the file contents match the file name. If the hash value does not match, MediaSentry relies on another piece of software, known as Audible Magic. The Audible Magic software attempts to download and play a segment of the song being shared. Using a method known as acoustic fingerprinting, Audible Magic compares the segment of the shared song to the fingerprint of the song listed by the file name. If the file name and file hash or acoustic fingerprint seem to indicate that the file actually is what it says it is, MediaSentry must then determine if the file is actually accessible. While other users accomplish this just by attempting to download the song, MediaSentry uses a different strategy. Instead of downloading the file, MediaSentry attempts to establish a TCP/IP connection to the computer sharing the file, verifying that the song could potentially be downloaded in entirety. In some cases, if neither the hash value nor the acoustic fingerprint matches the file name, a MediaSentry employee manually downloads the entire shared file and listens to it to verify the file contents. In this way, MediaSentry can determine if a given computer connected to the Gnutella network is sharing a file that

Is named similarly to a song listed in the RIAA list

Contains content that matches the file name

Is accessible to other members of the network

After these three pieces of information have been confirmed, MediaSentry then records the IP address of that computer, the files being shared by that computer that match the RIAA list, and the date and time at which the files were being made available. While the IP address does not directly identify the person who owns the computer sharing the files, it can be used to identify the Internet service provider (ISP) with which the Gnutella user has an account. Using a number of publicly available databases of IP addresses, MediaSentry can easily determine which ISP owns the IP address of the computer being used to share the files. Rather than attempting to actively identify all confirmed infringing P2P users to target them for lawsuits, the RIAA more frequently requests that the ISP send a warning to the users, allowing them to remain anonymous. However, in some cases, the RIAA chooses to target users for further legal action. First, the RIAA typically files suits against "John Doe" anonymous users in groups. At this stage, the users have not yet been identified, and an additional step must be taken to link an IP address to a name. Because the majority of ISPs (and college network administrators) keep logs of which accounts were using which IP addresses at specific times, the RIAA can then request that the ISP provide the name of the account holder who was using the IP address the RIAA recorded at the time the files were being shared. Typically, this type of request requires a subpoena from the RIAA. Once (or if) the ISP complies with the subpoena, the RIAA then has the identity of the infringing Gnutella user and may take further legal action.

In the case of college campuses, this process is fully automated. The software developed and operated by MediaSentry, combined with a list of 700 of the most popular songs from the RIAA/Billboard,[b] identifies infringing users, logs the information, locates the college campus from which the P2P traffic originated, and sends warning letters to the network administrators—which are typically passed on to the student who was using the identified IP address at the time of the infringement. When further legal action is initiated by the RIAA, the subpoena requests to the college campuses are automated in a similar way. The RIAA uses a different, larger list of songs for the litigation process, and once the infringing users are identified, they are then sent a message, allowing them to visit a Web page that processes prelitigation settlement arrangements. In these cases, the songs shared by the user are downloaded manually by MediaSentry employees, ensuring that the RIAA has obtained sufficient evidence to initiate legal action. However, this automated process is used solely to target infringing P2P use on college campuses and is not used to warn or identify P2P users who connect to the Internet through commercial ISPs. This is not to say that MediaSentry does not warn or identify these infringing P2P users, only that these cases are handled personally by MediaSentry employees, rather than through an automated process. Overall, through both the automated and manual processes, MediaSentry and the RIAA are capable of identifying hundreds of infringing P2P users every day.

You may have noticed at this point that there is no mention of the methods by which the RIAA identifies Gnutella users who have *downloaded* files that infringe on copyright. That's because currently, the RIAA (along with the majority of the major intellectual property stakeholders) does not target users who download infringing files, only those who make infringing files available through P2P networks. This is partially due to the fact that all potentially available methods to track downloading involve methods that may not hold well in a courtroom. This may allow some users who either share no files, or only share noninfringing files, to escape the view of the RIAA. This is largely due to the fact that from both a technical and a legal standpoint, monitoring downloaded files is extremely difficult. However, just because there is no current process to identify P2P users who download copyrighted files does not mean that one will not be developed in the future.

Notes

a. Catherine Rampell, "How It Does It: The RIAA Explains How It Catches Alleged Music Pirates," *Chronicle of Higher Education,* May 13, 2008, http://chronicle.com/free/2008/05/2821n.htm.

b. *Reuters,* "Inside the Music Industry's Piracy Battle," June 9, 2008, http://www.reuters.com/article/musicNews/idUSN0840383620080610.

for example, users attempting to download the new Harry Potter movie instead receive a file named "Harry Potter" containing nothing but 2 hours of blank video data. This process is known as spoofing files. While there have been no documented cases of any copyright holders actively sending files containing malware across P2P networks—doing so would place them under considerable, and unwanted, legal liability—there have been some incidents of spoofing in which copyright holders and artists have attempted to send messages to infringing P2P users through spoofed files. In one of the most publicized cases, after her album was found on P2P networks prior to its release date, in 2003, Madonna and her representatives flooded P2P networks such as KaZaA with spoofed files. These MP3 files contained a spoken message from Madonna, angrily asking listeners, "What the f— do you think you're doing?"[5] Obviously, this came as quite a shock to Madonna fans trying to download the album. While Madonna may have used spoofing to send a message directly to fans, the true purpose of spoofing is to make finding a spoofed file more likely than finding copyrighted content through P2P networks. Because a user can't know if the file is spoofed or real until the file has been downloaded, this can make file sharing significantly less easy and convenient. This particular tactic was quite popular through 2003 and 2004, but today, the amount of spoofing performed by copyright holders seems to have lessened to a certain extent—or at the very least, spoofing has become a less prominent impediment to file sharing.

In addition to spoofing, another tactic that prevents P2P users from downloading files is simple denial of service, or DoS. In Chapter 3, we discussed the weaknesses of the traditional client-server communication model. Because a single server can only handle so many requests from clients, with enough communication traffic, a server can be overwhelmed and shut down. This particular weakness is exploited by copyright holders in their fight against the illegitimate use of P2P networks. As we discussed, not all P2P networks are *truly* P2P, and many rely on centralized servers to perform specific tasks. These servers can be overwhelmed by too much traffic, just as any other server or computer connected to the Internet could be. By directing intense amounts of seemingly legitimate traffic at these servers, copyright holders can potentially slow down or shut down specific types of P2P networks. In particular, BitTorrent swarms are particularly vulnerable as the tracker systems that coordinate the file transfers are easily brought down by DoS attacks. Unlike sharing spoofed files, DoS attacks are in something of a legal gray area. As such, the use of DoS tactics is not frequently publicized and is generally kept secret. However, certain organizations are known to employ such tactics and occasionally attack the wrong target. One such attack, initiated as an attempt to slow illegitimate P2P traffic, accidentally brought down the Revision 3 Web site, an organization that specializes in video content development. The effects on the company were far reaching, disabling advertising, e-mail, and streaming video services.[6] Because of incidents such as this, where DoS attacks have been accidentally performed against legitimate services, this particular tactic has been widely criticized by system administrators and organizations that utilize P2P networks for legitimate purposes.

Both spoofing and DoS attacks, when used as anti-P2P tactics, are typically performed by a specific division of the copyright holder itself or by an outside technology firm contracted for the purpose. The most commonly used of these firms is SafeNet, which purchased and maintains the Media-Sentry suite of antipiracy applications. SafeNet, working with MediaSentry applications, provides automated monitoring, P2P user identification, spoofing, and DoS services. SafeNet's clients include the RIAA, among others. A second prominent firm that specializes in DoS and spoofing services is MediaDefender, which provides services to many of the individual member recording and movie studios of the RIAA and Motion Picture

Association of America. Not all attempts to manage P2P traffic originate from copyright holders or industry associations (and, by extension, anti-P2P service providers such as MediaSentry and MediaDefender), but rather from the ISPs themselves. Increasingly, ISPs have begun to filter, limit, and disable P2P connections as they traverse the Internet. The reasons cited by ISPs for engaging in such practices have primarily centered on concerns over P2P users consuming excessive amounts of bandwidth. ISPs manage P2P traffic through a variety of different technical measures. The most common is to use specific networking hardware to identify P2P traffic (usually BitTorrent) and throttle it, reducing the bandwidth available to that particular file transfer. Going one step further, ISP Comcast actively closed BitTorrent sessions that it identified for a period of time using an application known as Sandvine. Sandvine would actively monitor clients' Internet traffic for signs of BitTorrent use and, on identifying BitTorrent traffic, would send a forged reset packet to the computer that initiated that traffic. This reset packet essentially notifies the computer that the connection has ended, and no further communications will be sent, which disrupts any attempts to actually download or share a file. BitTorrent users that subscribed to Comcast Internet services quickly caught on, however, and filed complaints with the Federal Communications Commission (FCC). The FCC judged that such actions were in violation of federal communication policies, ordering Comcast to devise a different strategy for managing P2P traffic, effectively setting a precedent for any other ISP considering engaging in similar tactics.

USING P2P NETWORKS SAFELY (MOSTLY)

While this somewhat lengthy list of risks may seem somewhat daunting, in reality, safely downloading and sharing files through P2P networks is fairly safe and easy—with a little common sense and the right tools. After all, millions of people share files through dozens of different networks every day, despite the risks, and the wide majority of them have yet to experience any adverse effects. However, keep in mind that there is always some risk involved with downloading files through P2P networks—but this is largely due to the fact that you can't know the contents of a file until you have already downloaded it. And of course, anyone either downloading or sharing copyrighted files is immediately in violation of copyright laws and is therefore in danger of being targeted for legal action. No software tool, client configuration, or other method will change that. That said, there are steps that you can take to protect yourself and gain access to all the benefits of P2P with very little risk.

Using Antivirus and Antimalware Protections

All P2P users who download files are at risk of accidentally downloading malware. Luckily, after a few decades of development and revision, antivirus software is extremely easy to find and use. While it's far from perfect, antivirus software is the first line of defense against the more well-known threats posed by viruses, trojans, and worms. Unfortunately, not all antivirus solutions will also protect against other forms of malware such as adware and spyware. While some antivirus software developers are beginning to release more comprehensive malware defense solutions, others require additional layers of antimalware software, commonly known as antispyware. Luckily, there are freely available antivirus and antispyware solutions available for download. In combination, these two types of software provide a relatively strong defense against malicious software. Unfortunately, malware attacks are becoming increasingly complex, and antimalware developers are constantly struggling to stay one step ahead of the newest threats. There is no software in existence that can completely protect your computer against malware at all times, particularly if you download large amounts of content from P2P networks. There is, however, one more tool available to protect you from malware: a healthy dose of paranoia. Be choosy about how and what you download. First, try to stick with P2P networks that allow some means to rate or comment on users who share files. For example, torrent sites (which facilitate file sharing through BitTorrent networks; see the discussion on BitTorrent in Chapter 3) typically allow users to comment on each file available for download. Those that contain malware or spoofed content tend to receive negative comments by previous downloaders. The more information you can gather about the person or organization making the file available, the better. Of course, commenting on files or specific users is not always available on all P2P networks. When there is no additional information about a file you're trying to download, use the following tips to screen out potentially malicious files from your search results:

- Check the file name. How well does the file name match the file you're looking for? If the file name doesn't make any sense or is just a long string of popular-looking search terms—but contains the search term you searched for—there is a good chance that it contains malicious software.

- Check the file size. Does the size of the file seem to fit the content you're searching for? A single song in MP3 format is usually about 3 megabytes, and about two hours of video is typically compressed to no less than 700 megabytes. If a file seems small, avoid it. Attackers looking to spread malware commonly use smaller files, which consume less bandwidth. This becomes easier the more familiar you become with downloading files, which generally gives you a sense of how large specific files tend to be.

- Check the file type. Does the file type match the content you're searching for? Look at the last three characters of the file name, after the dot. This is typically known as the file extension and can be used as a method to determine what type of content a file contains. A common example is ".MP3," which lets both you and your computer know that the file should be opened as an audio file. Look at the extension on the file name before you download a file—if you're not sure what type of file it represents, use a Web search engine (like Google) to look it up. Always be wary of files that end in ".EXE," which are executable files or programs. If you are trying to download a song and you find a file ending in ".EXE," don't download it. Opening an ".EXE" file could execute a program that could do anything, ranging from a harmless prank to sending your personal information to an attacker.

Configure Your Client Software Properly

When you download and install a P2P client, make absolutely sure that it was properly configured. As we discussed previously, what you don't know about a file-sharing client *could* hurt you. Make sure to create a designated folder for downloading and sharing files and then configure your client to only download and share files using that folder. The proper configuration of your software can vary, depending on the network and client you choose. For the wide majority of P2P networks, on installation of the client software, you will (likely) be asked to set folders for downloading and sharing files. Not all clients will necessarily ask that you set these folders after installation and will instead use default settings. If this is the case, be sure to check the configuration manually to ensure that you are not accidentally sharing sensitive information. Never choose to share the entire contents of your hard drive, typically labeled as "C:\" on Windows-based operating systems.

Don't Download or Share Copyrighted Materials (or at Least Popular Ones)

This is a somewhat obvious step to avoid legal trouble while sharing files over P2P networks. Stay away from copyrighted materials, and you'll generally be safe. The chances that you'll accidentally download malware will go down, and you never have to be concerned that someone will catch you violating copyright law. If you follow this step, go ahead and skip the others listed later as malware protection and a properly configured client will provide all the necessary protection. Simply put, most of the risk from P2P file sharing comes from copyright holders protecting their rights, and the rest of these tips focus on avoiding detection while sharing copyrighted content. Now, despite my warnings, it has not escaped my attention that many of the readers of this book who use P2P networks ignore this step on a regular basis—and I imagine that the majority of the people who read this book will do so as well. I personally do not support downloading or sharing copyrighted materials, but if you absolutely have to, at least *avoid the most popular content.* While the lists of content used by the intellectual property industry to locate infringing P2P users are undoubtedly large, millions and millions of copyrighted works can potentially be distributed through P2P networks, far too many to track constantly. As such, these lists tend to contain the content that is worth the most, and the more popular intellectual property is, the more it is worth. Obviously, the contents of these lists are kept secret, so you can never know which files might be monitored, but the less popular a file is, the less likely it is to be monitored. Sharing the newest summer blockbuster is far more likely to make you a target for legal action than sharing an independent movie from the 1950s. Also, remember that there is currently no mechanism to target people who simply *download* copyrighted materials. I suggest avoiding both downloading and sharing, simply because there is a somewhat small possibility that there may be in the future. After all, a violation of copyright is a violation of copyright—the only difference between sharing and downloading is the possibility of being caught. If you're going to download copyrighted content regardless, some P2P clients allow users to disable sharing altogether. Check the settings in your client software to determine if you can disable sharing. Because the existence of P2P networks depends on users sharing files with each other, finding the option that disables sharing in client software is often deliberately made difficult to find, and for some networks (such as BitTorrent), sharing is required. Additionally, disabling or throttling sharing can often lead you to be temporarily or permanently banned from some networks, particularly those that require users to maintain a specific ratio of uploaded or shared data to downloaded data. If you do decide to share copyrighted files, do your best to remain as average as possible. Check the settings in your P2P client to see if you can prevent your computer from becoming a supernode, as discussed in Chapter 3. Share as little as possible for as little time as possible, and avoid facilitating additional infringing P2P use.

Use IP Blacklisting Software

To identify infringing users on a P2P network, copyright holders must first connect to the network and then attempt to initiate communication with users who are sharing files. Of course, this requires that they use an IP address of their own. Because the databases used by copyright holders to trace an IP address to an ISP can also be used to determine which blocks of IP addresses are owned by specific organizations, it is possible to create lists of addresses that might be used by copyright holders to connect to P2P networks. Theoretically, if it were possible to determine which IP addresses were bad ones used by anti-P2P organizations, a P2P user could simply tell his computer to block all communication with those specific bad addresses. On the basis of this concept, IP blacklisting software has been developed and is freely available online. This software blocks all outgoing communication with a large list of IP addresses belonging to intellectual property industry associations, government agencies, software developers, and movie and recording studios internationally to prevent P2P users sharing copyrighted materials from being identified. The most commonly used application is known as SafePeer, and additional blacklisting plugins are available for some P2P clients. Notice that I said that infringing P2P users could *theoretically* protect themselves completely; blacklisting is far from a perfect solution. Because both blacklisting software and the lists they use are freely available, copyright holders can gain access to them just as easily as P2P users can. Blacklisting has become a constant game of identifying potentially bad IP addresses and blocking communication with them, all while firms like MediaSentry do their best to appear as average P2P users, hiding their IP addresses using any means possible.

Avoid Large, Public Networks

Copyright holders and the companies that specialize in locating and identifying infringing P2P use cannot possibly monitor the entirety of each P2P network. Instead, they tend to target the largest, most popular networks. Just as sharing and downloading less popular copyrighted content will reduce the likelihood that you will be targeted for legal action, so, too, will sharing and downloading copyrighted content through less popular networks. Large networks open to the public, such as Gnutella, are prime targets for monitoring. Choosing to use a network that requires users to be invited or to register to gain access makes it far less likely that someone may be watching. Remember that the harder it is for you to gain access to a network, the harder it is for copyright holders to gain access to the network. Why expend the resources to gain access to a tightly controlled network of a few thousand infringing users, when there are millions connected to an easily accessible one? Many torrent sites have adopted this principle and often require that users be invited to join torrent sites by another user. Additionally, some P2P networks were originally designed only for use on college campuses and limit access to only those computers that have IP addresses on university networks. Just as with the other steps for safe P2P use (with the exception of step 3), joining a private network is no guarantee that you are completely hidden from P2P monitoring services—but it can lower the chances of being caught.

Don't Use P2P

Finally, if you are truly determined to download copyrighted material online, there is one more step that you can take to avoid detection: stop using P2P. While P2P is fast, easy, popular, and convenient, many of the older means of file sharing over the Internet are still going strong. Internet Relay Chat (IRC) and Usenet newsgroups are still popular means for distributing files—although not nearly as popular as P2P networks. As the number of P2P users sued by the intellectual property industry rises, many more technologically savvy file sharers have left P2P in favor of these older methods. However, there are many good reasons why P2P is far more popular than IRC and Usenet. Unlike P2P networks, IRC and Usenet have something of a steep learning curve, and the communities of users that populate IRC and Usenet are often unfriendly to "newbies" or "n00bs." Additionally, because IRC and Usenet are far less popular than IRC, ISPs often throttle traffic from these networks far more heavily. Some ISPs have discontinued service to Usenet altogether, citing concerns over child pornography. Despite the difficulties, using IRC and Usenet to download files is currently safe from the watch of copyright holders (for the most part). Like all of the other methods for distributing files, actively sharing content on IRC and Usenet can potentially increase your chances of being discovered. The laws change as an individual shares a specific amount of content—which we'll discuss more in Chapter 6—but for now, know that if you share large amounts of content over these networks, you will present a target not just for the intellectual property industry, but also for federal law enforcement.

IF YOU'RE A PARENT . . .

Not everyone is in the enviable position of being the only computer user in her household—or even being in control of the computer she uses on a daily basis, for that matter. If you're a parent, it's likely that you have children in your household who either share your computer and Internet connection or have computers of their own. If this is the case, after reading about all of the risks associated with P2P use, you may not be entirely sure whether or not your computer is being used for some form of online piracy. If this is the case, and you're not sure if your children (or other household members) are using P2P programs to violate copyright, it is in your best interest to find out. Because copyright holders cannot determine precisely who is using a computer when they determine their copyrights are being violated online, they target the only person they can identify: the person associated with the ISP account. If you pay the Internet connection bill, and someone in your household uses your Internet connection to violate copyright, you are the one at risk. What can you do?

Just Ask!

While it may not always be the most effective method, particularly as awareness about online piracy grows, simply asking the other people in your household if they use P2P networks, and how they use them, is certainly one of the easiest methods you can use to determine your risk. Talking about what it is that your children or household members do online is always a generally good idea, and asking about P2P use is no exception. The fact of the matter is that not everyone who uses P2P networks to download and share copyrighted works immediately recognizes that what he's doing could potentially land him (or you!) in legal trouble. By talking about it, you can decide as a family what you see as appropriate computer use. Besides, immediately going to the computer and uninstalling suspicious-looking programs can often send the wrong (somewhat antagonistic) message and might lead whoever is using those programs to search for ways to hide them from you. So ask about P2P use and talk about it before doing anything else.

Do Some Investigating

Even if you're not all that much of a power user, doing a little computer sleuthing can be easy. Start by taking a look at the computer your child or household members use the most. If you can't get access to that computer, try starting out with the first tip given in this chapter. When you get access, start by looking at what programs are running—do any of them look like they are P2P clients? Do some poking around: check through the applications installed on the computer and see if any of them match the names listed in Chapter 3. Windows users can do this by clicking the "Start" button and browsing through programs, and Mac users can simply look for the "Applications" folder on the hard drive. Additionally, browse around the file system to see if you can locate folders that are labeled "Downloads" or "Torrents." Find out what is in those folders, and ask yourself if the contents might be copyrighted. Is the hard drive mysteriously full? P2P downloads, particularly pirated movies and software, can take a very large amount of hard drive space. Even check the desktop for shortcuts to programs that might be P2P applications. One way or another, these programs are not typically designed for covert operation—they're usually out in the open somehow, so you should be able to identify them with a little detective work. Unfortunately, if you choose to start deleting these programs without talking to the people who use them first, it's likely that you'll end up causing them to hide their P2P use. If you're someone without strong technical skills, this could quickly become a problem for you, so remember to talk with the other people in your home about what you find.

Watch for Music, Movies, and Software of Unknown Origin

Finally, be on the lookout for new music, movies, and software. In particular, if you see someone watching a movie that is currently in the theater, it's a safe bet that the movie was obtained illegally, somehow. If the origins of the content can't be easily explained, or if you happen to notice a large amount movies and music being transferred about on writable CDs or DVDs, it might be a good idea to be a little suspicious. That said, just because you see someone in your home burning a CD doesn't mean you should immediately accuse her of online piracy. But if you see a lot of new music or movies whose presence can't be easily explained, it might be a good idea to ask where they came from.

Overall, it's up to you to discuss what is and is not considered appropriate computer use with your family. Becoming involved in how your children use computers and the Internet is the best defense against the risks associated with P2P. Yes, there are technical fixes, but there are also technical workarounds to those technical fixes that are particularly simple for users who have physical access to the computer. Talk about computer use with your family, and then monitor computer use to be sure that the agreed on rules are followed. As a parent or guardian, you are the first line of defense.

SUMMARY

Do you really want to be safe on P2P networks? Stay away from copyrighted content. That's really all there is to it. But if you absolutely have to mix P2P and copyrighted files, at least try to stick with downloading it. Most of the risks associated with P2P networks come from the intellectual property industry, and for now, everything else can be avoided fairly easily. That said, it's not as bad out there as I might make it seem. A little common sense goes a long way to keep you protected online, and even if you choose to share copyrighted content over P2P networks, the probability that you'll be targeted for legal action is very small. As we'll discuss in the next chapter, there are millions of users across dozens of file-sharing networks, and despite the fact that the tally of civil lawsuits brought about is in the tens of thousands, the chances of any one user being singled out of millions is still miniscule. That said, there is undoubtedly that small chance that you'll be targeted, and an even larger one if you're on a college campus in the United States. Ultimately, everyone decides how much risk she's willing to accept to gain access to free copyrighted materials online. Always ask yourself before firing up your favorite P2P client, how much risk am I willing to accept?

Chapter 5

EXTENT AND EFFECTS
OF ONLINE PIRACY

Everyone knows that there are millions of pirates out there on the Internet, swapping millions of dollars' worth of music, movies, software, and any other form of intellectual property that can be converted to a digital format. And with all those millions of pirates sharing millions of copyrighted works, the intellectual property industry is losing millions of dollars on all of the lost sales. In fact, much of what has been covered in this book so far has assumed that there are large numbers of people involved in online piracy—if nobody was doing it, would it be worth writing a book about? In Chapter 2, I discussed how thousands of new users began pirating software with each change in computer and networking technology, particularly when those changes increased the speed of computer networking, increased digital storage space, or made computers—and by extension, the software/hardware that facilitates piracy—easier to use. In Chapter 3, I described how P2P networks effectively become stronger as more nodes join the network. Even Chapter 4 assumes that there are enough people using P2P networks to present an attractive target not only for computer criminals, but additionally for the intellectual property industry. But is it enough to assume that there are millions of online pirates, or, for that matter, that the changes brought about by P2P networking are largely negative? In this chapter, I'll provide a more detailed look at the *nature and extent* of online piracy, along with a discussion of how the use of P2P networks for a variety of purposes has played a role in the shaping of the intellectual property industry, information technologies, and society. More specifically, this chapter will provide an overview of the studies that have been performed in an effort to measure online piracy and its effects.

STUDYING ONLINE PIRACY

Unfortunately, actually measuring the prevalence of online piracy is not as easy as one might think. Nobody has a magical Internet wand that can simply measure all the online pirates at any given moment. Pretend for a moment that you have been asked to do a study measuring the extent of online piracy via P2P networks. Here you are, with thousands of dollars in research grants and with a team of researchers at your side. Where do you start? What do you do? On the surface, it may seem like an easy task, but as it turns out, measuring online piracy is actually an extremely complex problem. Knowing what you know from Chapter 3 about how P2P networks work, how would you begin counting infringing P2P users? Would you connect to a P2P network and do a search for a file, and count the number of nodes that return a result? If so, you've just managed to count the number of users on one network sharing a particular kind of file—and there's no way to be sure your search request reached all the connected nodes sharing files of that type. What if you managed to gain access to a segment of the Internet that handled a significant amount of network traffic and then somehow were allowed to monitor that traffic (a procedure known as network sniffing) for P2P use? If so, you could not be entirely sure that your segment of the Internet was representative of all the others, and it is likely that you would lose the ability to determine if any given P2P session actually represented an act of copyright infringement. OK, then, what if you avoided the P2P networks entirely and just decided to do an online survey about piracy behavior? As with any other survey, your data would be self-reported by each individual respondent, who could lie or misinterpret your questions, and how could you know that your sample of respondents is equivalent to the general pirate population? More important, what would you ask, and how would you ask it? You may get significantly different answers depending on only slight changes in the wording of specific questions. How do you define a single act of piracy? Is it downloading a file? Uploading one? A single hour spent participating in a BitTorrent swarm?

Researchers face all these methodological questions when attempting to gain a better understanding of the nature and extent of online piracy, or any other phenomenon, for that matter. All of this isn't to say that it's impossible to measure online piracy in a meaningful way—some have attempted it and have been fairly successful in doing so—but I do want to highlight that each method of measurement has various strengths and weaknesses. Depending on which method you use to measure online piracy, you'll end up with a very different view of what the online piracy problem is. Then again, it's quite possible that you may not view online piracy as a problem at all. One would think that with the attention that online piracy has received over the past few decades, there would be a large amount of research being done on the topic. However, because it can be so technically difficult, relatively few researchers have made an attempt to actually determine how much online piracy is occurring or what it is people do when they choose to download and share copyrighted material online. As with any other potential problem, we need to know two things: what is happening out there, and how much of it is actually happening? Only once we have the answers to these questions can we start to determine if there is a need for further action, whether it be new regulation, changes in technology, educational programs, or shifting business models. Because the varying views of online piracy may lead us to make different decisions about how we might address the problem, we need to be very careful about how we evaluate the results generated by studies of online piracy. As we run through the studies that have been done on online piracy, and as you read any studies on online piracy in the future, try to keep the following questions in mind.

What Are They Really Measuring?

A wide variety of activities might be placed under the digital piracy umbrella. These activities could range from copying a song from a CD you own to your computer, all the way to hosting a warez server containing millions of dollars' worth of copyrighted software. The concept of piracy is really too big to be measured in any one study, and depending on where a researcher chooses to draw the boundaries, the results will look different. So find out precisely what counts as piracy for each study and try to think about whether or not it fits with your personal definition of piracy.

How Did They Obtain Their Data?

Because piracy is such a broad concept, a researcher might choose to gather data regarding piracy in a number of different places, using a variety of methods. It truly would be impossible to measure it all, so researchers usually only choose one or two methods for gathering data. Where, when, and how they choose to do this is extremely important. Anybody could ask a few people on the street whether they pirate music, but would you then use that information to write legislation? Probably not. Look at the methods that the researchers chose to use and try to determine if the tiny pieces of the online piracy puzzle they examine are strong enough to tell us something about the world of online piracy as a whole.

Who Are They?

Who actually did the research, and why? Different researchers will make different research decisions for different reasons, and those decisions will end up influencing the end results. Did the Recording Industry Association of America (RIAA) pay for the study? Is the researcher an ex–music pirate? While you shouldn't dismiss a study entirely on the basis of its affiliations, its affiliations might justify being a little more suspicious. Who a researcher is will invariably become part of what she chooses to study, how she chooses to study it, and how she will interpret the results, so knowing something about the researcher can help you understand why she says what she does.

What Work Does This Study Do?

Of the five, this question is probably both the most important and the most tricky. In the ways in which each researcher chooses to talk about his subject of research, there are hidden assumptions. You need to try to see through what is being said and unpack those assumptions when you look at any scientific research. Think of it this way: how does the way in which the researcher presents his findings change our view of the subject, and what would the subject look like if the findings were presented differently? As an example, let's try to unpack the phrase "Video game addicts are less active than avid readers." First, the phrase implies that there is a clear difference between video game addicts and avid readers—what if those groups overlap? Second, it assumes that it is possible to be a video game addict. Finally, merely by using the word *addict,* video games become something that are dangerous and unhealthy in comparison to reading. Don't take statements by researchers (or anyone) for granted; rather, unpack them.

Could I Find Enough Information
to Answer All These Questions?

Sometimes finding enough information to answer all these questions can be difficult. Not all researchers release information to the public for free, particularly when they are contracted to do studies for private organizations. While being unable to answer any of these questions does not necessarily invalidate any one study completely, it is a good reason to be a little cautious with how you choose to interpret the results. What might they be hiding by not giving you all the answers? Although I won't be providing you with all the answers—this chapter alone could likely fill an entire book—keep this in mind when you review research for yourself.

Given all this all-too-academic information on studies and such, you may be wondering why I don't just toss some statistics at you and be done with it. For one, I've already described how fuzzy all this research can actually be. Some of these studies directly conflict with one another but offer equally valid perspectives on online piracy—perspectives you should probably know about and evaluate for yourself if you're trying to educate yourself on the topic. Any summary I make will obviously trim those perspectives down quite a bit and would not be nearly as rich compared to all the studies in depth. Second, to understand online piracy, as the title implies, you'll need to know how the tensions between the intellectual property industry and media consumers play out in the research and take a stance for yourself. Just because I've already done that doesn't necessarily mean that I should make that decision for you. Finally, a few statistics from me would make for an extremely boring (and short) chapter. That said, if you are not interested in wading through this information for yourself, skip ahead to the end of the chapter for the down-and-dirty summary. For those of you who want to really know what it is that we claim to know about online piracy, press on.

GENERAL P2P USE

While P2P certainly can be (and is frequently) used for purposes beyond those that involve copyright infringement, it would be somewhat safe to assume that a significant amount of P2P use violates copyright in one form or another. Starting with that assumption, we can use studies that measure the extent of P2P use to get a sense for how big piracy really is online. One of the best sources is, of course, the sites and networks that support P2P. As of 2009, the Pirate Bay, one of the world's top two largest BitTorrent trackers, hosted 1,377,015 torrent files shared by 15,058,195 peers (users) globally.[1] Mininova.org, another torrent site in constant competition with the Pirate Bay, indicates that BitTorrent users download approximately 8 million torrent files from its site and upload 3,500 new torrents every day. This means that on Mininova alone, approximately two new torrent files are uploaded to the site every minute, and 100 are downloaded every second.[2] While torrent files frequently overlap between sites, and P2P users undoubtedly participate in multiple torrent swarms simultaneously, this still represents a huge number of users, even before counting users of the other popular networks such as Gnutella and eDonkey.

BigChampagne, a private research firm that specializes in tracking P2P usage, has been gathering data online since 2000. Specifically, BigChampagne markets its data to analysts and media producers who want to know how specific content is being consumed online. While the reports generated by such an organization typically are difficult to obtain without spending quite a bit of money, P2P news site Slyck.com published statistics from BigChampagne on the average number of simultaneous P2P users between August 2003 and September 2006. This means that BigChampagne constantly attempts to count how many users are connected to all of the P2P networks at the same time at any given moment. Globally, these data indicate that within this time period, the number of P2P users rose somewhat steadily, with a few exceptions, moving from 3,847,585 users in 2003 to 9,044,010 users in 2006. In the United States, the increase in average users has been far more consistent, rising from 2,630,960 to 6,986,980 users in (January) 2006. Interestingly, the most significant drop in the number of average users in that time period occurred between October and November 2003, falling from 3,764,032 average users to 2,498,431 average users in the United States. This would seem to lend support to the conclusions that a private research firm drew from its survey of Internet users: the announcement made by the RIAA that it would begin suing P2P users had a significant effect on American P2P use. However, this effect was short-lived. Only two months later, the average number of P2P users had risen back to where it was before the announcement and continued to rise from there. Despite additional announcements of P2P lawsuits, only the first had any major impact, according to BigChampagne.[3] As with many private research firms, BigChampagne tends to keep its research methods confidential, so we can't be sure exactly how it goes about counting these millions of users. But in general, methods used simply to count and track P2P users tend to be at least somewhat successful—particularly because there are no sticky concepts to try and operationalize. Using the data generated by both BigChampagne and the Pirate Bay, it seems somewhat reasonable to assume that the trend toward higher numbers of simultaneous users has continued since 2006.

In another more recent collaborative analysis done between BigChampagne and PCPitstop, 1,661,688 computers were checked for P2P software as part of an antimalware scan provided by PCPitstop. These scans were performed approximately every six months between September 2006 and September 2007. According to the last data point given by the report in fall 2007, the two most popular P2P clients installed on the computers sampled were LimeWire, a Gnutella network client, and uTorrent, a BitTorrent client. It was found that 36 percent of these computers had Limewire installed, while 11 percent had uTorrent installed. In the United States, only 17 percent had Limewire installed, and 2.1 percent had uTorrent installed. However, the study found other varieties of P2P client, in addition to Limewire and uTorrent, and these two forms of P2P client represented only half of the P2P market share. In comparison to 2006, this indicated a trend away from Limewire, with 6 percent fewer installs, and toward uTorrent, with 3 percent more installs on the sampled computers. These data additionally indicate that the Gnutella network is still the most popular, followed by BitTorrent and eDonkey, and demonstrate a slow drain of users from the FastTrack (KaZaA) network.[4] Even with such a huge sample of PCs being examined, these data, too, have their limitations. While this type of scan can determine if P2P software is installed, it cannot determine whether, or how frequently, the software is being used.

Finally, Sandvine, a company that develops networking equipment that scans and shapes network traffic, released a report on the amount of P2P traffic on the Internet in May 2008. Sandvine performed this study by going to an undisclosed number of American broadband Internet service providers (ISPs) and monitoring Internet traffic. This report indicated that P2P represented 36 percent of all downloading traffic and 75 percent of all uploading traffic, representing an aggregate of 45 percent of all Internet traffic. This percentage of Internet outweighs Web browsing, media streaming, and online gaming. The percentage of P2P traffic is greater than that of any other form of traffic on the Internet, according to Sandvine's analysis. Additionally, this represented an increase from the percentage of P2P traffic Sandvine measured in a similar study performed in 2007, which indicated that P2P use was only 40 percent of Internet traffic.

HOW BIG IS ONLINE PIRACY?

Given what we know about how much P2P use there is online, how can we determine the extent to which P2P is being used for copyright violation? As we know, computer users have been engaging in digital piracy for decades, going all the way back to copying paper tapes with the instructions for MITS Altair BASIC in the 1970s. But it wasn't until the late 1980s, after computer crime began to solidify as a public concern, that researchers first began paying attention to software piracy. The first researcher to do so was a criminology professor at the University of Florida, Richard C. Hollinger, who, in 1989, conducted the first study on computer crime and abuse. Hollinger chose to use a survey to measure digital piracy, which would become the primary method for such studies. Hollinger's study focused on only two dimensions of computer abuse, unauthorized access and software piracy, and only asked participants if they had engaged in those behaviors within a period of four months. Of the 1,672 student participants from an American university, 10 percent reported having received or given a pirated copy of commercial software from or to someone else. When Hollinger extrapolated these results across the entire student population, it was calculated that there were 3,500 incidents of felony piracy occurring at the campus under study every four months.[5] While 10 percent may not seem like much of a problem, keep in mind that in 1989, the personal computer was far less ubiquitous than it is today, and sharing files over the Internet had only just become a possibility given hardware and bandwidth constraints. Although there are no other studies that measured the population outside the college campus from which Hollinger drew his sample, Hollinger's study seems to further indicate that piracy was a common behavior at universities even before digital music and digital video were available to students. Despite the widespread adoption of computer and Internet technologies that placed digital piracy increasingly within the grasp of the average computer user, and the crackdown on pirate bulletin board systems throughout the late 1980s and early 1990s, the next academic attempt to measure digital piracy didn't occur until 1997. Following Hollinger's example, a pair of researchers, Skinner and Fream, performed a second study of computer crime with 581 students at another American university. This study not only expanded on Hollinger's original questionnaire by measuring more than two forms of self-reported computer abuse, but it also attempted to determine a theoretical explanation for computer abuse. Unsurprisingly, a high prevalence of self-reported software piracy was found, with 41.3 percent of respondents admitting to using, copying, or giving away pirated software.[6]

At this point, if you are asking yourself the questions I listed earlier, you may have noticed something of a trend. Both studies were done by college professors, on college campuses, with groups of (mostly) undergraduate students. Unfortunately, the population on the majority of college campuses does not generalize well to the world population. While studying the piracy behaviors of college students might tell you something about piracy on college campuses, it probably won't tell you all that much about digital piracy out in the world. Researchers justified their work by mentioning that college campuses, even then, were seen as centers of digital piracy to an extent, so these studies did provide some useful information—particularly for increasingly concerned college administrators. And because it is convenient for college professors to study college students (samples gathered in this way are often called *convenience samples*), there are actually quite a few studies on software piracy that followed those of Hollinger and Skinner and Fream. These studies, as convenience studies on college campuses with extremely small numbers of participants, compose the majority of academic work done to measure digital piracy behavior and are very limited in their usefulness. I'm not going to cover them all here—there are too many, and a few hundred college students just can't tell us very much about what's happening out there. I do, however, want to mention them because anyone looking into piracy (either online or traditional) is bound to stumble on them, so keep a skeptical eye out.

During the late 1990s and early 2000s, the majority of data on software piracy came from the software industry itself. The Business Software Alliance (BSA) and Software Publishers Association (now subsumed by the BSA) have completed their own software piracy studies. It was, after all, their software being pirated. Rather than surveying computer users, the initial studies done by these associations in the 1990s were originally based on computer and software sales. By combining information on the number of computers sold, the amount of software sold, and the average number of programs installed on each computer, the associations made estimates on the total number of pirated software installations. These studies assumed that if the total number of installed programs across all sold computers was greater than the total amount of software sold, then the difference between those two totals must be the number of pirated software installations. Using this method, in 1994, the SPA estimated that 49 percent of all software was pirated globally, while 31 percent of all software was pirated in North America, which was the lowest rate across all of the regions examined.[7] By 2000, the global piracy rate, according to the BSA (using the same method), had actually fallen to 37 percent.[8] The advent of P2P file sharing failed to increase the falling software piracy rate, and according to the BSA, by 2005, global piracy rates were down to 35 percent, while the North American piracy rate had actually fallen to 22 percent.[9] Finally, in 2007, the global piracy rate rose to 38 percent, while the North American rate again fell to 21 percent.[10] All these studies, based completely on sales data, fail to distinguish between online software piracy and traditional software piracy. The programs on computers could have come from anywhere and could be the result of traditional piracy or simply free, legal software. The data provided by the BSA do have one interesting point to make about online software piracy, though. Despite the rise of easy-to-use P2P networks and software, software piracy, as measured by the BSA data, continued to fall. This would appear to indicate that the widespread adoption of P2P has had little, if any, impact on software piracy rates.

However, this methodology was not the only one used by the BSA to examine software piracy. In 2002, the organization began to administer surveys to Internet users in an effort to measure the amount of online software piracy. The results were released under somewhat misleading headings such as "Survey Spotlights Growing Problem of Online Software Piracy," despite steadily falling overall software piracy rates. These surveys, which were given to both Internet users and college students, appear to reflect the national piracy rate—but without a detailed description of how the information was collected, it can be difficult to determine what it was that the surveys actually measured.[11] Why would the BSA suddenly switch to survey methods, then announce the "Growing Problem of Online Software Piracy"? Your first clue should be in the timing. In 2002, P2P file sharing had been growing consistently, causing increasingly more headaches for the music industry. In addition, P2P networks were beginning to branch out, increasingly offering content other than just music. The BSA was gearing up for a fight with the ever growing swarm of P2P users, even if its own data indicated that online software piracy was on the decline. Always remember that it's easy to make statistics say what you want them to say, and there may be interesting reasons for doing just that. The BSA seemed to begin reframing its surveys in a more conservative way, as P2P file sharing failed to increase the piracy rate over the following years. In 2007, the BSA released the results from a series of surveys specifically targeting youth Internet users. The data from these surveys again indicated a steady reduction in the amount of online software piracy among Internet users aged 8–18, falling from 22 percent in 2004 to 11 percent in 2007.[12] Overall, the BSA data seem to indicate that software piracy, whether online or offline, has been in decline for at least a decade.

While studies of online music and movie piracy do not quite have the history that the studies of software piracy have, music and movie piracy has certainly drawn more attention by scholars and the public. Of course, prior to the adoption of the MP3 music format and Napster, online music piracy wasn't much of a concern, and few computers could manage to play digital video compressed enough to transfer between computers on the Internet. In 2000, as the Napster network continued to grow, everyone began talking about online music piracy, and some recognized that online movie piracy was likely to be just as important. As Napster became part of mainstream conversation, and the RIAA started to publicly announce its concerns, scholars began to recognize online music piracy as an interesting topic of study. In the early 2000s, research began to be published on the online music piracy phenomenon. Unfortunately, these scholars faced the same problems that those who attempted to measure software piracy did. As I've said before, nailing down online piracy in a meaningful way is extremely difficult—even when researchers narrow their focus to a single type of piracy—and as such, each study seemed to take different views of what was actually happening online. These studies were primarily about the impacts of file sharing on the intellectual property industry and will be discussed in further depth later on.

A private research firm, the Pew Internet and American Life Project (or, simply, Pew), was the first to release a study concerning the extent of online music piracy in 2000. Conducting a telephone survey of 2,503 American adults (including 1,345 Internet users), Pew determined that 14 percent of Americans (approximately 13 million) were engaging in at least some form of free music downloading. Pay close attention to that last sentence and try to figure out what might be problematic about it—go ahead, take a minute. If you answered that "music downloading doesn't have to be piracy," you are absolutely correct. How many times in your Internet lifetime have you ever legally downloaded a song for free? Pew, attempting to operationalize online music piracy, asked Internet users if they "downloaded music for free." That music could have been anything, from anywhere online—there was no indication that the act of downloading somehow violated copyright. However, in addition to surveying Internet users, Pew also routinely logged on to the Napster network in an attempt to determine how many people were actually sharing files. After a month of sampling, Pew determined that approximately 5,000 users were connected to each indexing server, sharing a total of 500,000 songs each. When scaled out to Napster's claim of 10 million users, this indicated that the Napster network contained approximately 1 billion (nonunique) files.[13] As the drive for more information about online music piracy increased, Pew continued to perform similar surveys. According to its results, the percentage of adults engaged in music downloading rose to 22 percent later that year, and again to 29 percent in early 2001. This percentage remained steady until November 2003, when it was recorded that only 14 percent of American adults were engaged in music downloading. Pew indicated that this large drop was due to the announcement of civil lawsuits being brought against file sharers by the RIAA.[14] Interestingly enough, the BSA survey performed in 2007 (mentioned earlier) also asked respondents about both music and movie piracy, in addition to software piracy. The results indicated that in 2004, 53 percent of 8- to 18-year-olds engaged in online music piracy. By 2006, this percentage had fallen to 32 percent, and even further to 30 percent in 2007. Movie piracy was found to be significantly lower, with only 17 percent engaged in the practice in 2004, later dropping to 10 percent in 2006 and to 8 percent in 2007. Unfortunately, the BSA also chose to operationalize online piracy by describing it in terms of "downloaded without paying"—so just as with the Pew studies, these statistics are at least somewhat questionable.

Another, lesser-known private research firm, Ipsos-Reid, also conducted a major study on online piracy, focusing specifically on college students and P2P use. The survey was provided to 1,000 college students and 300 college faculty and administrators in 2003. In my opinion, this survey was extremely well designed, and the questions asked by the survey administrators did an excellent job of developing questions that actually measured online music, movie, and software piracy via P2P networks. Somewhat unsurprisingly, when asked if they had ever even heard of P2P networks, 95 percent of the students answered that they had, while only half of the faculty and administrators had. This was, of course, prior to the announcement that the RIAA was going to begin suing P2P users on college campuses. The survey then asked students if they had ever downloaded music, movies, or software through a P2P network—keep in mind here that the "ever" time period is broad, and we don't know how much or how frequently the students used P2P networks to obtain copyrighted content. In response, 69 percent of the students admitted having downloaded music, while only 26 percent indicated that they had downloaded movies, and 23 percent indicated that they had downloaded software. Additionally, approximately 30 percent of students indicated that they would always download music or movies through P2P networks if it saved them money.[15]

One other smaller survey, again conducted by a private research firm—Nielsen NRG—on behalf of the Motion Picture Association of America (MPAA), is worth mentioning here. This survey, conducted in 2004, specifically targeted Internet users with children between the ages of 12 and 17, resulting in 396 respondents. While small, this study did result in a number of interesting findings. First, "nearly 40%" of the parents surveyed indicated that they were unaware that sharing copyrighted material via P2P networks was illegal. Furthermore, "more than 40%" indicated that they knew their children downloaded music and movies over the Internet, and of those, 55 percent knew the content was not paid for. Perhaps most interesting was the finding that one-third of the parents who used P2P (the percentage of parents who did so was not released) had learned to do so from their own children.[16]

Many of the largest survey research projects on computer crime phenomena to be produced by academia were managed by Samuel McQuade through the 2000s. In the interest of full disclosure, I personally worked on many of these research projects along with McQuade, so take that for what you will when you consider who it was that performed the research. These studies, like many of the studies that had come before, asked college students about a variety of computer crime offenses and experiences. These studies were different than the other studies of online piracy on college campuses for a number of reasons, however. First, the number of students who participated in the studies was much larger and more closely representative of the student body of the campus being studied. Second, these studies were performed at a college once described by members of the warez scene (see Chapters 2 and 3) as one of the two mother ships that kept the scene running.[17] In particular, this campus had an extremely high bandwidth connection to the Internet, making it ideal for couriers to quickly move files between warez sites. Of course, it made the campus ideal for those interested in using P2P networks as well. So the campus where these studies took place was a hotbed of online piracy, representing a worst case scenario for copyright holders. In the first of these studies, over 800 students were asked about their participation in and experiences with a wide variety of computer crime behaviors, including music, movie, and software piracy. Unfortunately, the way we chose to ask about "how much" piracy students were involved in was somewhat ambiguous. A year later, in April 2005, McQuade was asked to perform another study of online piracy, following the adoption of a new legal music service made available to students at the same university. The wording of many questions designed to measure piracy was changed, and the instrument was provided to both users of the new legal service and nonusers of the service. Of the students who responded to the survey, half were users of the service and half were not, for a total of 442 responses. Nearly 96 percent of the respondents responded that they had a basic understanding of P2P file sharing, and half admitted to currently using a P2P file-sharing application to share music. Of those who admitted to currently using a P2P application to share music, half (25% total) did so at least once per week. When asked about the number of songs that they had downloaded within the past year, 48 percent of the P2P users responded that they had downloaded more than 100 songs, indicating that once individuals become P2P users, the majority of them download large volumes of songs. By multiplying the number of users who responded within each response choice by the highest and lowest numbers of songs downloaded listed for that response choice, it can be estimated that within this sample alone, between 14,265 and 18,540 songs had been downloaded through a P2P service within the past year. When extrapolated across approximately 15,000 students attending the school, between 470,745 and 611,820 songs are downloaded through a P2P service per year. If we assume that 120 songs is the maximum considered for the "more than 100 songs" response, and that nearly half of the participants answered in that category, these estimates are highly conservative. Of particular interest in this survey was the fact that no statistically significant difference in P2P use between users and nonusers of the legal service was found, effectively indicating that people who downloaded music from the legal service used P2P networks just as frequently as those who did not, even when the service was available for free.

A second, even larger study, also a collaborative effort between McQuade and me, measured computer crime phenomena experienced by 40,079 kindergarten through 12th-grade students in the Rochester, New York, area from May 2007 to January 2008. In this study, the survey was administered to the entire population of some school districts, representing the largest study ever conducted on the topic. Of course, given the age of some of the younger cohorts of students, it was not possible to ask all students directly about online piracy. However, students between 4th and 12th grade were asked about downloading music and movies online. When fourth- to sixth-grade students (8,632) were asked if they had downloaded content online "without paying for it" within the past year, 8 percent responded that they had downloaded music, while 3 percent indicated that they had downloaded movies. At the seventh- to ninth-grade level (10,366 students), 22 percent of respondents indicated that they had downloaded music and 9 percent indicated that they had downloaded movies, while 13 percent indicated that they had shared music and 7 percent indicated that they had shared movies. Again, while we aren't entirely sure that these activities are actually piracy, it would be difficult to dismiss these results as entirely legitimate downloading and sharing. Finally, the 10th to 12th-grade instrument actually measured "illegal" downloading behavior within the previous year. Of those who responded to the survey (6,500 students), 65 percent indicated that they had pirated music online, 34 percent indicated that they had pirated movies online, and 30 percent indicated that they had pirated software online. While this survey does not indicate the amount of content being downloaded and shared illegally by these students, these results certainly indicate that it is a behavior in which many students engage at least occasionally.[18]

EFFECTS ON THE INTELLECTUAL PROPERTY INDUSTRIES

Now we have a sense that millions of people are online at any given moment, sharing millions of copyrighted files containing all forms of content across all the countries of the world. Online piracy is big, but many of us already knew that. Just take a look at your own friends and family; I bet it won't take too long until you find a pirated copy of Windows XP, a DVD rip of the biggest new movie, or an iPod full of copied MP3s. The real question is, so what? Generally, we know that individual file sharers must think piracy is a pretty good deal—there are, after all, millions of return customers every day. We also know that the intellectual property industry hates it—they tell us every opportunity they get, through the media and their own litigious actions. Regardless of what everyone thinks and wants, we can't just assume that online piracy is either beneficial or detrimental without some kind of proof, as much as people on either side of the digital copyright debate would like us to do so. Besides, things are never as simple as they seem, and online piracy is most certainly an example of that. The research done on online piracy effects reflects this, and some studies directly contradict one another. Further confusing the issue, many industry studies tend to lump traditional piracy—where physical copies of media (like DVDs and CDs) are sold for profit—with online piracy. These are two very different activities and may have very different effects on legitimate sales. Intellectual property industry associations tend to gloss over this distinction, immediately assuming that every pirated copy, whether it is bought on the street or freely copied online, is the equivalent of a lost sale. Piracy in any form is, in their minds, theft. Whether you agree with the stance that piracy is theft, if you've ever engaged in online piracy yourself, or if you know people who have, it's likely that you know from experience that piracy does not always translate into lost sales. What about people who own the CD and just want easy access to MP3s? What about those who download an album and purchase it later? On the other hand, once you've bought a physical disc (either music or movies) of some sort, will you ever decide to throw it out and go buy a legitimate copy? Probably not, if you've already spent your money somewhere else. So it bears repeating that you should always be sure you know what type of behavior is being measured in a study: is it traditional piracy, online piracy, or both?

While software piracy is certainly the oldest form of online piracy, few have actually attempted to gauge its effects on the industry. Of course, the annual BSA Global Piracy Study has certainly generated statistics on the financial impacts of piracy, with the last estimate being a total of $40 billion in losses worldwide. In 2007, the U.S. software industry alone lost $8 billion to software piracy, more than any other country in the world. Unfortunately, we already discussed the fact that the BSA study is based entirely on discrepancies between the average number of installed programs on a computer and the amount of software sold. The BSA isn't entirely concerned with dividing piracy between traditional and online forms— and why should it be? Lost sales are lost sales, and by muddling the two together, the problem becomes even bigger. However, the BSA study does take note of the fact that between 2008 and 2012, 700 million people are expected to become Internet users, and 200 million households are expected to gain access to broadband Internet connections. As history has shown us, as more people gain access to faster Internet connections, the capacity to pirate software (and other content) increases. What the study does not discuss is the expected degree to which piracy rates will increase due to new Internet users, some of whom will undoubtedly become new online pirates. Despite the fact that the method by which the BSA gathered these data is somewhat weak, most of the academic studies on the effects of online software piracy (or just software piracy) were based primarily on these data. This meant that most of these studies were complex economic studies, using financial models to estimate the damage done to the industry, rather than attempts to actually measure these effects through some form of observation. In my opinion, these types of studies are just as weak as the data provided by the BSA and unsurprisingly echo the alarming tone that the BSA uses to discuss it findings, so take them with a grain of salt.

The first academic studies on the effects of music piracy began to trickle in during the early 2000s, as music sales data became available. Most of these studies were similar to those performed by the software industry in years past: economic analyses of industry data. The first was performed by Stan Liebowitz in 2003 as an attempt to give some form of grounding to ongoing policy discussions about online piracy and file sharing. Liebowitz begins by noting that between 1999 and 2000, music sales data indicate that music sales dropped by approximately 5 percent and continued to fall into 2002. Of course, Napster began to gain widespread acceptance during this period of time. Liebowitz effectively compares and combines industry data from a variety of sources and concludes that the sales drop is due largely to the popularity of MP3s and Napster. However, by his own admission, the case made by Liebowitz on such a basis is "far from airtight."[19] Given the rising popularity and urgency of the topic of online music piracy, other researchers began taking up the problem as well. All using a variety of different data resources and perspectives, these studies indicated that new phenomena of online music piracy accounted for a drop of between 7.8 percent and 12 percent in U.S. music sales between 1999 and 2003, representing billions of dollars of damage to the industry.[20]

However, one study disagreed with the findings put forth based on economic data. One of the most widely cited studies (by those outside the industry) on the impacts of online music piracy was performed by researchers Felix Oberholzer-Gee and Koleman Strumpf in 2002 and published in 2004. Rather than choosing to survey P2P users, or to rely solely on industry sales data, Oberholzer-Gee and Strumpf were some of the few who chose to actually monitor the traffic on a P2P network. Arguably, this study provided the most comprehensive look into P2P use and effects, and there is a lot of information to cover. The two researchers constructed and maintained an indexing server on the then second most popular file-sharing network, OpenNap, and then used the logs from that server to determine the amount of online music piracy over a course of 18 weeks. At the time, OpenNap was developed as a replacement for the then defunct

Napster network, but without the central points of control. As an indexing server, the logs generated allowed the researchers to determine the IP addresses (and therefore the locations) of P2P users, in addition to the search terms they used and the files they eventually chose to download. These data were then compared with both music sales data and academic calendars, including vacation schedules. Through the period of 18 weeks, over 1.75 million file downloads were logged—approximately 10 per minute—representing an estimated 0.01 percent of all the P2P downloads during that time. On the OpenNap network, there were 3 million files available to approximately 5,000 users at any given point in time. This snapshot of P2P use was incredibly detailed, allowing Oberholzer-Gee and Strumpf to track the habits of individual users over time, all over the world. P2P users in the United States were responsible for 36 percent of all downloads, downloading 260,889 audio (song) files. By checking the logs against a database of songs based on the top 575 albums of 2002 (comprising 81.8% of CD sales that year), only 47,709 (18%) matched. Somewhat unsurprisingly, the most downloaded files came from the tops of the music sales charts. However, Oberholzer-Gee and Strumpf also calculated that it would be necessary for an album to be downloaded via P2P networks 5,000 times to reduce the sales of that album by one copy. Again, using the data generated by the OpenNap servers, it was estimated that P2P music piracy resulted in a loss of 2 million albums every year. Given that the music industry sold 803 million albums in 2002, and that the drop in sales between 2000 and 2002 was 139 million, 2 million albums is a relatively small amount for the music industry as a whole. By these calculations, Oberholzer-Gee and Strumpf conclude, P2P music piracy has only an extremely small (and statistically insignificant) negative effect on music sales. Additionally, because P2P file sharing increases free access to media, they argue that it likely increases the aggregate welfare of P2P users and those who benefit from their downloading.[21]

Oberholzer-Gee and Strumpf additionally used their data to attempt to determine the behavior of the average P2P user. Interestingly, the average user was only observed over a period of two days and downloaded 17 files. Basically, the average P2P user only used the P2P network for two days every three months, to download the equivalent of one or two albums. Not all users used the network so infrequently, and the top user was observed over 71 days and downloaded over 5,000 files. Additionally, a relationship between school vacations and amount of files on the network was found, meaning that as schoolchildren went on vacation and had more home computer time, the participation and number of files on the network went up.

Obviously, the conclusions drawn by Oberholzer-Gee and Strumpf caused quite a controversy, particularly because their results were being picked up by the mainstream media. Liebowitz and the others held their ground, however. The three researchers were placed on a panel at a special P2P workshop convened by the Federal Trade Commission, and an argument erupted that threatened to drown out the other presenters.[22] Mentioned during this workshop by Liebowitz was another study being done using a similar method as the one used by Oberholzer-Gee and Strumpf. This study, performed by David Blackburn and published in 2006, compared sales data for the top albums with file-sharing data generated by BigChampagne. BigChampagne is a private research firm that tracks the popularity of content on P2P networks, usually at the request of clients such as the RIAA and MPAA. It does so by logging on to the network and searching for keywords, then using that data to estimate how many files matching that keyword are available across the network as a whole. This differs from the method used by Oberholzer-Gee and Strumpf in that their data allowed them to track the actual behavior of specific users through the network, while Blackburn's method only allows access to the number of files available on the network at any given time. Although Blackburn specifically mentions that he believes the number of downloads and the number of files on the network to be relatively equivalent as far as his theoretical model goes, personally, I'm not at all convinced that they are. In the end, Blackburn came to the opposite conclusion of Oberholzer-Gee and Strumpf, determining that online music piracy has strong effects on music sales. Specifically, Blackburn focused on estimating the effect that removing files (and users) from P2P networks would have on album sales. He concluded that by reducing the number of files available in 2004 by 30 percent, the recording industry could have increased profits by $261 million—a 7.9 percent increase.[23] Additionally, because Blackburn was actively collecting data as the RIAA announced its first round of lawsuits, he was able to draw conclusions about the effect of the announcement on P2P use and album sales. He determined that following the RIAA announcement, album sales rose by 2.9 percent, leading to increased profits of $1,616,370 per week.

Strangely, despite the fact that the RIAA was extremely concerned over the potential of P2P networks to cause financial harm to the music industry, it released no online piracy statistics to the public. It may have been conducting private studies of online piracy in secret, but it primarily relied on steadily declining sales data to indicate that P2P use was impacting the industry. However, the RIAA merely pointed at the sales data and then suggested that there was a relationship between the rise in P2P use and the decline in album sales. While it may appear that these two are related, without any additional analysis, we cannot immediately assume that they are. Further confusing the situation, the RIAA frequently cited statistics on the rise of traditional piracy under the label of "piracy." While the press releases would typically suggest that traditional piracy and online piracy were distinct behaviors, and additionally, that actual statistics on online piracy are extremely difficult to generate, the tactic of confusing the two was a successful one. Regardless of whether the rise in P2P use was actually causing harm to the industry, publishing press releases that indicated that "piracy" was on the rise and doing billions of dollars in damage certainly drew public attention to the issue. This isn't to say that piracy *wasn't* causing any damage: the possibility that it was, and would continue to do so, was a very real one, so taking defensive action was a valid response from the industry. And why wouldn't the RIAA want to tie a potentially significant threat to the music industry to the highly organized criminal activities of traditional piracy? Unfortunately, this also means that there are no real statistics on the financial effects of P2P use from the organization in one of the best positions to gather them: the recording industry itself.

Just as with the studies that focused primarily on how much piracy was occurring, the focus began to shift away from the effects of online music piracy, particularly as personal computers began to become capable of playing increasingly higher quality digital video and high-bandwidth Internet connections became increasingly popular. With this increased capacity to create, play, store, and transfer digital video, the motion picture industry began to take notice of online video piracy. While the MPAA frequently published press releases citing financial losses due to piracy, these press releases commonly fell into the usual pitfall of lumping traditional piracy and online piracy together. However, in addition to these press releases, the MPAA also released statistics from studies of its own. In 2005, the MPAA released the results of a commissioned study to determine the impacts of both digital and traditional piracy on movie sales. This survey was surprisingly broad in scope, surveying over 20,000 people across 22 countries under the direction of the research firm LEK. This study estimated that the U.S. movie industry lost $6.1 billion in 2005 alone. Of this $6.1 billion, 20 percent, or $1.3 billion, was estimated to have been the result of piracy in the

United States. The worldwide movie industry, including movie companies outside of the United States, was estimated to have lost $18.2 billion. Ah, but wait! Here, again, we find that not all is what it seems. These multi-billion-dollar figures are the result of the total amount of piracy, combining both traditional and digital forms. In the published results for this particular study, the MPAA actively admits that the two are combined, but of course, this makes for a much more impressive figure. When separated out, it was estimated that only $2.3 billion was lost due to online piracy among the U.S. companies. By comparison, these totals represent far smaller sums of money, yet still enough to run a small country or two. Unfortunately, as is the case with many studies initiated by the intellectual property industry, it is not clear how exactly the dollar losses were calculated, or how an instance of piracy was measured. By way of explanation, they state simply that "piracy loss calculation is based on the number of legitimate movies—movie tickets, legitimate DVDs—consumers would have purchased if pirated versions were not available."[24] This pushes us again into the problem of knowing when a sale is lost. However, if other industry statistics are any indicator, it is likely that it was assumed that an instance of piracy was equivalent to a lost sale.[25]

While the attempts by the RIAA to call attention to music piracy were largely successful, leading many academic researchers and private research firms to begin to examine the nature of online music piracy, comparatively few researchers began to examine the newer phenomenon of online movie piracy following alarming press releases from the MPAA. In effect, this means that we know very little about the effects of online movie piracy, although statistics on traditional movie piracy are released by the MPAA fairly frequently. Part of the reluctance to study online movie piracy may be due to the consistent trend of increasing yearly box office sales. With the exception of 2005, total box office gross has risen annually since 1992. Additionally, 2007 was a record-breaking year for the movie industry,[26] and DVD sales have been largely on the rise since 1997, all of which would at least somewhat indicate that online piracy has had at most a limited financial effect. That said, if we assume (as the intellectual property industry often does) that each pirated copy of a movie is equivalent to a lost ticket or DVD sale, the question then becomes about how much *more* the industry *could* have made had online pirates not had access to the movie at all. Then again, just as with the Oberholzer-Gee and Strumpf study on online music piracy, it is almost certain that online movie piracy represents some form of net good to consumers. Should the movie industry get all the money they are entitled to under the law, or should the consumer be allowed to benefit from continued violation of copyright? These are difficult and controversial questions.

Ultimately, we know very little about the *current* effects of P2P on the intellectual property industries. It is undeniable that online piracy has had some negative financial effects, and the research that has been done places the damages between hundreds of millions and billions of dollars. How those damages are interpreted and reported by stakeholders and legislators is a different and more complex question. What does and does not represent a social problem, worthy of legislative and educational efforts? While losing a few hundred million dollars may seem nearly unthinkable to an individual consumer, this may potentially represent a mere scratch to the global intellectual property industry. Of course, for the industries losing money, annual scratches might eventually become fatal wounds, so interpreting what we do know in such a way that portrays online piracy as a significant problem only makes sense. However, the issue of positive and negative effects of online piracy is far more complex than mere industry profit. Do consumers benefit from online piracy in some way? Do artists and developers? How does piracy shape or break our conception of copyright law, and does it do so in a way that is helpful or harmful to us as a society? At the very least, millions of P2P users obviously gain something from sharing and downloading copyrighted works online, and as such, the definition of online piracy as a problem is hotly contested. As such, there will continue to be industry press releases describing P2P users as "thieves," and there will continue to be discussions by P2P users describing the industry as "evil." You need to decide for yourself what you think of online piracy and where you fall between the extremes of online piracy as a problem and online piracy as a net good. Is your online piracy glass half empty or half full (and whose drink is it)?

SUMMARY

So, after all of that, what do we (think we) know about online piracy? Most of the data are expressed as a percentage of Internet users who have at some point engaged in online piracy—or at the very least have downloaded something at some point in their lives. Keep in mind that measuring online piracy in such a way glosses over some important information but is better than nothing. Overall, having been looking at studies such as this for nearly a decade now, and without pointing to any specific study, I'm generally left with the sense that online piracy is on the rise and that it's not doing as much damage to the industry as the industry would have us believe. That said, you have some evidence here in front of you now, an entire Internet full of interesting bits of information on online piracy, and (most important) your own experiences with your family, friends, and colleagues—you be the judge of whether online piracy represents a threat. Make your own decision. But for those of you who skipped to the end of the chapter and are just looking for some quick statistics, here they are.

How Many People Are Using P2P Networks?

- By any count, millions. In 2006, BigChampagne estimated that there were 9 million P2P users globally, 6 million of which were located in the United States. One of the largest BitTorrent sites, the Pirate Bay, boasts 15 million users connected to its trackers alone as of fall 2008.
- The number of P2P users appears to be on the rise, based on information from BigChampagne and statistics from BitTorrent trackers.
- P2P use represents nearly half (45%) of Internet traffic, more than any other form of Internet traffic, including Web browsing, media streaming, and online video games. (This does not indicate, however, that P2P use is "clogging up the Internet tubes.")

What Do We Know about Online Software Piracy?

- Data on online software piracy are limited, but what we do have seem to indicate that software piracy is on the decline. A survey done by the BSA indicates that 22 percent of youth Internet users indicated that they had pirated software online in 2004, while only 11 percent said the same in 2007.
- In a survey of Rochester area students, 30 percent of 10th- to 12th-grade students indicated that they had illegally downloaded software within the past year.
- Industry sales data indicate that software piracy as a whole (including traditional piracy) is declining steadily in the United States, down from 31 percent in 1994 to 21 percent in 2007. In other countries, such as Russia and China, a higher percentage of software piracy exists and has not been reduced as quickly as in the United States, in addition to increasing global piracy rates.
- Again based on industry sales data alone, software piracy (again including traditional piracy) is costing the software industry billions of dollars every year. The most recent report estimates that a total of $40 billion has been lost to software piracy, with $7 billion lost in 2007.

What Do We Know about Online Music Piracy?

- Taken in aggregate, the private studies seem to indicate that approximately 15 to 20 percent of the U.S. population engages in online music piracy of some form but that this percentage has been declining since approximately 2003.

- Among the younger generations, particularly those in high school and college, music piracy is more prevalent. Approximately 25 percent of college students use P2P networks to download music, and more than half of 10th- to 12th-grade students indicate that they illegally download music. More students pirate music via P2P networks than pirate movies or software.

- The largest study performed on the effects of P2P music piracy, and the only one that actually monitored P2P use, indicates that one album must be downloaded 5,000 times before resulting in a single lost sale, and that the financial effects on the music industry by P2P users is small and statistically insignificant. Additionally, this same study indicates that online music piracy represents a net benefit to the consumer that outweighs the damage to the music industry.

- However, nearly all of the economic analyses (based on industry sales data, as opposed to measuring P2P use) indicate that P2P is actually doing significant damage to the music industry. These studies indicate that online music piracy accounted for a drop of between 7.8 percent and 12 percent in U.S. music sales between 1999 and 2003, representing billions of dollars of damage to the industry.

- Another study, which measured the number of files available on P2P networks, indicated that by reducing the number of files on P2P networks by 30 percent in 2004, the music industry would have made an additional $261 million in sales—a 7.9 percent increase.

What Do We Know about Online Movie Piracy?

- In 2005, the research firm LEK estimated that the U.S. movie industry had lost a total of $2.3 billion to online movie piracy.

- Three percent of fourth- to sixth-grade students and 9 percent of seventh- to ninth-grade students indicated that they had downloaded movies online "without paying for it" within the past year. Thirty-four percent of 10th- to 12th-grade students indicated that they had illegally downloaded movies within the past year.

- Little beyond the LEK study is known about the financial impacts of online movie piracy, but the movie industry has posted record box office sales throughout the past decade, seemingly indicating that any damage that is being done will not cripple the industry anytime soon.

If you haven't found what you're looking for in the statistics I've provided here, or if you just want additional information, see Appendix B. There you will find links to academic studies, press releases, and media coverage. There's more to the online piracy phenomenon than simply millions of P2P users and an unknown quantity of financial damages, however. Online piracy is changing the way we understand and consume our media across the world. New business models are being developed, new technologies are entering the market, and the ways in which we produce and distribute media are changing, all as a result of the rise of online piracy. Coming up in the next chapter, I'll be describing some of the ways in which online piracy has changed, shaped, and become a part of (or maybe already was a part of) our cultures.

Chapter 6

DIGITAL COPYRIGHT LAW

It has been my experience that most people only have a vague notion of what copyright is and why it came about, let alone why breaking it might not be a good thing. I get a sense, however, that this has started to change, particularly as Internet users are increasingly able to publish content of their own online and as organizations such as the intellectual property industry and the Electronic Frontier Foundation attempt to increase public awareness of copyright issues. Still, many people just aren't sure what does and does not constitute a violation of copyright. In this chapter, I'll be providing a guide to (primarily U.S.) copyright law and how it constrains and enables various forms of online piracy. As I mentioned in the introduction, I am not a lawyer, and the information in this book *should not* be taken as legal advice; if you need legal advice, find a lawyer. Before we get into issues of digital copyright law and policy, first, I would like to step back into history just one more time. Some observant readers may have noticed that in Chapter 2, I avoided discussing the history of how and why legislation developed together with computer crime and online piracy. Instead of discussing the history of online piracy, here I'll be describing the history of copyright. To begin a (Western) history of copyright—which is also, of course, a history of the violation of copyright—we'll have to go back much further than the 1970s, all the way back, in fact, to just before the invention of the printing press itself, in the early 1400s.

THE HISTORY OF (DIGITAL) COPYRIGHT

In Europe, prior to the invention of the printing press, literary works were tightly controlled by religious organizations. Few were literate; nobles would hire at least one servant with the ability to read simply so that he could interpret written messages. Roman Catholic churches employed the wide majority of the literate population as monks, who would spend years copying books by hand. As such, most written works were, unsurprisingly, of a religious nature. The written word and the ability to read and write were perceived by many as miraculous. The illiterate majority relied heavily on memorization, witnesses, and symbols for record keeping in the absence of written, permanent documents that could be universally read. The written word was distrusted for such purposes as documents could easily be forged—after all, if you can't read the record yourself, the person reading it to you could be lying to you. Little thought had been given to the rights of the authors prior to the invention of the printing press, primarily because the tedious nature of copying books limited the number of copies that could be made, given constraints on time and resources. Even if one were to take the time and effort to make one or two copies of a book by hand, how would the original author possibly know about it? Instead, those who owned a printed version of the text itself were given compensation for the right to copy it. In any case, only so many copies were likely to be made within the lifetime of the author of the text, all of which would be incredibly difficult to track down by the original author. Furthermore, copyists were trained in handwriting as an art to be interpreted, rather than as a set of rules to which the copyist should rigidly adhere. Each copy of a work could be seen as a unique work unto itself, with changes in spelling, grammar, and style according to the individual skill and whim of the copyist.[1]

The invention of the printing press is most frequently attributed to Johann Gutenberg, a goldsmith during the early 1400s. However, the basis for the printing press can be traced back to China, far before the appearance of the printing press in Western societies. Originally derived from woodblock prints, a number of Chinese printers tried various combinations of block material and ink composition, with limited success. The major difficulty for the Chinese printers was in the language itself, rather than the materials that were chosen for the printing process: there were simply too many different characters to sort through and manage. While the extent to which the Eastern attempts at printing had any effect on the Gutenberg press is unknown, it seems highly unlikely that Gutenberg was entirely unaware of the Eastern techniques. Gutenberg's true invention was not that of the press itself, but rather that of a printing system. The exact combination of linseed oil-varnish ink with metal type and wooden hand press, free of the inherent barrier of a logographic writing system, was what led to such extreme social and technical changes throughout the world.[2] The widespread adoption of the printing press brought major changes in the ways information was distributed all over the globe. Books could now be accurately reproduced by the thousands, without any loss in quality. Each copy of a printed work was exactly the same, in both style and content. As the power to print and distribute literary works was brought to a larger number of people outside the Church, less secular texts were made available to the public at a lower cost. Even more important, the amount of effort and time that went into each copy of a book was significantly reduced. Thousands of copies could now be printed in the time that it took a calligrapher to transcribe one, making book copying a far more profitable endeavor.[3]

Before copyright regulations were put into place, publishers relied primarily on secrecy to ensure that the authorized publication of a work would be the first to the market. By 1525, unauthorized versions of the German Lutheran bible were being reproduced at 90 times the rate that Martin Luther alone could produce them. More out of the fear that widespread access to uncensored literary works would lead to rebellion than of concern for intellectual property rights, the English monarch Mary I granted exclusive printing rights to a select group of printers, known as the Stationers' Company, in 1556. This was not true copyright law but did lay the foundation for later regulations. This system failed to prevent unauthorized printers from continuing to make illegitimate copies of books. In fact, many of the authorized printers would themselves illegitimately copy books and profit from their sales. Book piracy became ubiquitous throughout Europe, as printers forged licenses and printers' marks. After nearly 200 years of infringement on authors' and printers' rights, Queen Anne passed the Statute of Anne in 1710, which is commonly accepted as the first comprehensive copyright law. Unlike the formation of the Stationers' Company, the Statute of Anne focused on ensuring the protection of authors, rather than on censorship of works deemed unacceptable by the government. This statute gave the legal claim of ownership to either the author or someone who had arranged to obtain the rights from the author. The legal ownership lasted 14 years, which could be extended to 28, before the property lapsed into the public domain, allowing anyone to copy and sell the work. With the exception of the time limits, this law looked much like the one we have adopted today in the United States.

Only a few decades later, in 1775, the American Revolutionary War began in North America. When the dust had settled, the Americans emerged with the American Constitution in 1789. The power for the American government to create statutes was written directly into the Constitution:

> The Congress shall have power . . . to promote the Progress of Science and useful Arts, by securing for limited Times to Authors and Inventors the exclusive Right to their respective Writings and Discoveries. (Article 1, Section 8)

This provided Congress with the constitutional power to create copyright laws to protect authors and inventors, acting as a form of incentive to produce new works and ideas. After all, why should authors and artists develop and publish new ideas and works, only to be sold by the pirates, without profit to the original developer? So, in 1790, Congress adopted a law providing protection to American authors and cartographers, which were both technologies that relied on printing for copying. The system of copyright protection provided by American law was nearly identical to that provided by the British Statute of Anne, establishing a balance between the rights of the author and the needs of the consumer. However, there was one major exception: the American Constitution writers recognized the financial potential of the intellectual property industry and granted protection only to works by American authors. By omitting protection of copyright holders in countries other than America, the American government essentially legalized the unauthorized copying of foreign works. This omission allowed the American publishing business to grow rapidly and successfully, primarily by purchasing copies of European manuscripts prior to their publication in Europe, then publishing them in America. It was within the publishers' best interests to flood the market with copies of these books to ensure that the competition did not do the same. With so many copies available on the market, reducing the protections given to foreign authors under American copyright effectively provided the newly formed nation inexpensive access to some of the best entertainment and research in the world. For example, Charles Dickens's *A Christmas Carol* was sold for merely 6 cents in America, as opposed to two dollars and 50 cents in England.[4] Arguably, this access helped to drive economic growth as well. Of course, all of this came at the cost of the welfare of authors in other countries, something that foreign governments did not entirely appreciate.

In 1886, a gathering was held in Berne, Switzerland, including representatives from all the major European nations. The value of what was then known as literary property (as opposed to intellectual property) had been apparent for quite some time, and the intent of the meeting was to form an agreement to protect copyright on an international scale. The majority of the attending nations signed the agreement, which provided copyright protection to foreign authors as if they were citizens. Not all nations agreed to the Berne Convention, however. The United States, while invited and in attendance at the convention, failed to sign the agreement. At the time, sheet music was extremely popular as the only method of transporting music from place to place beyond human memorization. Capitalizing on the American copyright laws, publishers would print sheet music by European composers, then export those copies to the European markets. America was sharply criticized for not signing the Berne Convention, but doing so was not in the interest of the American markets. The protection of foreign authors and composers within the United States failed to be an issue for American copyright law, until the number of American works rose significantly, forcing American authors to seek copyright protection in other countries. Finally, in 1891, American copyright law began to cover works by foreign authors.[5] However, it would not be until 1988 that Congress would actually approve participation in the then 102-year-old Berne Convention.[6]

As I mentioned earlier in Chapter 2, in the early 1900s, England was also facing a national piracy problem with sheet music, particularly as pianos came into popularity, despite the creation of the Stationers' Guild, which controlled what could be printed and by whom. Despite the law, sheet music pirates would print out warehouses full of inexpensive sheet music, similar to those copies sold in America. Of course, this forced the authorized publishers of sheet music to compete with the sheet music pirates. At this time, copyright law protected sheet music, but the sheer volume of the problem made enforcement difficult for legitimate publishers. Publishers formed roving sheet music enforcement squads, organizing illegal, but acceptable, raids on the pirates and burning entire warehouses full of pirated sheet music. In 1902, changes to the law placed enforcement of copyright within the penal code, allowing police officers to enforce what had previously only been a civil matter. The police found it difficult to enforce the copyright law, particularly with the support of the public being on the side of the pirates. The public viewed the illegitimate printers as a check on the music printing industry, preventing sheet music prices from being artificially inflated, a practice common among the legitimate printers.

Early copyright law followed the widespread adoption and use of the printing press, as first European and then American governments recognized the value of protecting authors from the unauthorized copying and distribution of their work, as the use of the printing press itself forced legislators to reexamine methods of controlling the flow of information, while protecting the rights of authors and artists (see Figure 6.1). As such, each developed copyright laws that were somewhat unsurprisingly similar to each other. Between then and now, the basic tenets of copyright law have gone largely unchanged, primarily providing protection of specific author rights within a specific time frame. What did change, however, were the types of works that copyright protected. The original American copyright law, as specified in the Constitution, lasted just over 100 years before new technologies forced legislators to consider additions and has faced many revisions and additions since that time due to technological advancements. Of course, these technological advancements were all devices that either changed the ease and cost by which one could make a

Figure 6.1. Patent consultant advertisement offers to protect authors and inventors from pirates.

copy, or the methods by which those copies could be distributed, or both. The law was amended to protect works developed with each new form of communication technology, including photography in 1865, works of fine art in 1870, and translations of works in 1870. This trend continued through the decades, with the last major change occurring in 1976 with the Copyright Act, providing the United States with the law under which we operate today. However, many new communication devices have been made available to the public within the past few decades, including audio cassettes, video cassettes, CD recorders, and DVD recorders, each placing additional tension on copyright law and often creating similar patterns of copying behavior to that following the adoption of the printing press.

It is hoped that all of this history is looking at least slightly familiar, assuming you have read through Chapter 2 or are at least slightly familiar with online piracy and the actions of the intellectual property industry. Like the printing press and the myriad new communication technologies that followed, the widespread adoption of computers and the Internet has placed significant tension on copyright law, driving additional legislation, congressional hearings, and action by law enforcement and the intellectual property industry. It wasn't just the adoption of these technologies that drove these actions, however; rather, it was the widespread use of them for the purposes of copying and distributing copyrighted works in digital form. Here again we find an overwhelming number of people, all of whom find copyright violation acceptable to a certain degree, using a new technology to make cheap and more accurate copies in a more efficient manner. This time, it isn't sheet music printers making warehouses full of unauthorized copies, but P2P users making additional copies of music with each download on a massive scale; it isn't roving bands of publisher enforcement squads armed with torches policing the pirates, but the Recording Industry Association of America (RIAA) and the Motion Picture Association of America (MPAA) suing individual P2P users. Even before P2P use, however, people were using the Internet to share valuable intellectual property through bulletin board systems (BBSs) and FTP sites, causing legal concerns that led to legislation that protected software and digital works under copyright.

As I mentioned in Chapter 2, by the 1990s, the software industry was beginning to take the growing digital piracy problem more seriously as well. The pirate BBS scene had largely peaked, and software pirates were flocking to the commercialized Internet, abandoning bulletin boards for FTP servers and Internet Relay Chat (IRC) systems. In 1993, a student from the Massachusetts Institute of Technology (MIT), David LaMacchia, used several MIT computers to host a pirate BBS known as Cynosure. Noticing the unusual behavior, and the large amount of communication traffic generated by the system, MIT notified the Federal Bureau of Investigation. Following an investigation, LaMacchia was eventually indicted on one count of violating the wire fraud statute, which prohibited the use of interstate lines for fraudulent purposes. The prosecutors on LaMacchia's case had no other option—at the time, creating and distributing copyrighted works in digital form was not yet illegal under copyright law. After just over a month of operation, the government estimated that the Cynosure BBS system had been used to illegally distribute more than $1 million worth of software. Despite the value of the software itself, the indictment failed to cite any financial gain on the part of LaMacchia during the BBS operation. LaMacchia was charged by the government under the wire fraud statute, but LaMacchia's defense argued that the wire fraud statute did not apply to the case due to the lack of financial gain or commercial advantage. Furthermore, the defense argued, interpreting the wire fraud statute to protect copyright would render it unconstitutionally vague. The judge accepted the defense's argument and dismissed the case, much to the anger and frustration of the federal prosecutors. The dismissal of the LaMacchia case, along with the threat that digital piracy posed to the software industry, led software copyright owners to seek the assistance of Congress. Congress first responded by passing the No Electronic Theft (NET) Act in 1997. Until this time, copyright law was designed to punish those who duplicated copyrighted works for financial gain, allowing those who gained nothing financially while infringing on copyright to slip through the legal system. In the act, the definition of financial gain was modified to include the receipt of anything of value, including copyrighted works, and criminalized the duplication and distribution of works valued at over $1,000. While the act was specifically designed to close the LaMacchia loophole, specifically targeting the administrators of large pirate servers, it was ineffective in reducing piracy rates, despite a number of convictions in the years that followed.[7] In a sense, the NET Act was similar in timing and effect to the creation of the Stationers' Guild in the 1500s. While the NET Act successfully led to the prosecution of approximately 80 software pirates, including a number of high-profile piracy group members, the rate of piracy continued to rise even during the time the cases in violation of the act were being prosecuted.[8] Furthermore, the seemingly more serious crime of piracy for commercial gain went largely unnoticed. Similarly, the creation of the Stationers' Guild following the development of the printing press—an initial attempt at protecting the copyright of authors and publishers—also failed to reduce piracy, and again, the printed piracy rate actually increased during this time.[9] However, in both cases, the actions taken were initial attempts at protecting copyright in the face of changing technology, and more restrictive legislation was to follow.

Despite the fact that the NET Act was found to be largely unsuccessful, it did play an important role in the history of digital copyright law. The NET Act became a stepping-stone of sorts, and having learned from the deficiencies of the NET Act, Congress began working on new digital copyright laws. What followed in 1998 was one of the most controversial pieces of copyright legislation: the Digital Millennium Copyright Act, or simply, the DMCA. The DMCA was a direct result of what was effectively a modern Berne Convention—the World Intellectual Property Organization[10]—and was developed to implement in the United States two of the treaties set forth by this organization. The DMCA is currently the single most important piece of legislation concerning digital copyright in the United States, and given the borderless nature of the Internet, it has significantly impacted Internet users around the globe. The DMCA was designed to manage the new threats created by the increasingly widespread adoption of the Internet: the cracking of copyright protection mechanisms, the unauthorized publication of copyrighted works on the Internet, and the production of digital copies of works. Additionally, the DMCA marked a shift in the way in which Congress viewed the balance of power between the artist and the consumer. The DMCA was passed within a week of one other addition to copyright law: the Sonny Bono Copyright Term Extension Act. This act extended the length of time that works are covered under copyright, keeping them out of the public domain (which makes them freely available to all), by 20 years—making the total amount of time most works are covered equal to the life of the author plus 70 years. Combined with the DMCA, the Copyright Term Extension Act clearly tipped the balance of power toward authors and copyright holders. Due to this shift in the balance of power, and the potential chilling effects on research and creativity that result from the way in which the law was written, the DMCA has been widely criticized.

Following the DMCA, the most recent significant change in digital copyright came in October 2008, when the Prioritizing Resources and Organization for Intellectual Property (PRO-IP) Act was signed into law. As the name suggests, as a law championing intellectual property (instead of the public domain), the PRO-IP Act further increases the amount of protection provided to artists and copyright holders. The law further increases the penalties for copyright infringement, provisions for the seizure of goods from those in violation, and creates a new cabinet position: the intellectual property enforcement coordinator. Prior to being passed, this law broadened the protections provided to authors and copyright even further, granting federal law enforcement the ability (and therefore a level of responsibility) to prosecute civil copyright infringement cases, but this provision was eventually removed due to concerns that law enforcement would waste valuable time acting as copyright cops.

WHAT COPYRIGHT LAW MEANS FOR P2P USERS

Each one of these laws, from the 1978 Copyright Act to the carefully titled PRO-IP Act of 2008, changes the legal environment in which online piracy takes place in the United States. As such, each comes to bear on the practice of online piracy, ranging from obtaining unauthorized prerelease copies of a work, all the way to sharing files through a P2P network. These laws regulate cyberspace, delineating what is and is not acceptable use of copyrighted material online. What does all this mean to you as an Internet user—or possibly a P2P user? Well, before we get into that, first, you'll need to know a little something about the way the law works and the different types of laws that apply to digital copyright and online piracy. Throughout the previous chapters, I have discussed raids and sting operations carried out by federal law enforcement officials against online pirates—actions that are used to target criminals. On the other hand, I've described the process by which the RIAA and other copyright holders might locate the Internet protocol (IP) address of a P2P user and use this information to sue (or settle with) the person it believes to be in violation of copyright—with no law enforcement in sight. So what is the big difference? Why are there police officers banging down the doors of some online pirates, but not others?

As it turns out, different levels of copyright violation are handled differently in terms of punishment. These forms of punishment fall into two categories: civil and criminal. The emphasis in criminal law is the punishment of an individual found in violation of the law through fines or incarceration, while civil law focuses primarily on the reparation of damages done to the plaintiff of the case. Another difference between the two types of law lies in who is responsible for gathering and providing evidence of copyright infringement to the court. Where the copyright holder is responsible for gathering evidence and presenting a case in civil copyright infringement lawsuits, the federal government is responsible for those actions in criminal copyright infringement lawsuits. Finally, the standard of proof is greater in criminal cases than it is in civil cases. In civil trials, the standard of proof is based on a "preponderance of evidence," which requires only that the weight of the evidence be greater for either the plaintiff or defendant. In criminal trials, the prosecutor must prove her case "beyond a reasonable doubt," which is the highest standard of proof. This difference has become particularly important when handling online copyright infringement, given the difficulty of obtaining evidence of infringement, making the civil trials more amenable toward the arguments brought by the intellectual property industry against P2P users. The general rule of thumb is that small-scale copyright violation is typically covered by civil law, whereas large-scale copyright violation involving thousands of dollars' worth of content is typically covered by criminal law. As such, the broad majority of copyright violation cases fall under the category of civil law such as those cases brought by the RIAA against individual P2P users. Because of the amount of government resources required to investigate and prosecute a criminal copyright infringement case, such as the LaMacchia case I mentioned earlier, they tend to be far less commonplace than civil copyright infringement cases.

Always keep in mind that the law does not provide a solid, clear dividing line by which judges may quickly and easily determine the guilt of a party, particularly in cases involving digital copyright. Instead, laws are frequently vague, and in each case, judges determine whether a given law is applicable based on the evidence provided by each party. Through the decisions made in each court case, judges further define the law with increasing detail, a concept known as legal precedent. So in the areas in which a law does not clearly define whether or not a given behavior is in violation, by ruling in certain ways and setting a legal precedent, judges have the power to shape the law through practice. More often than not in digital copyright cases, the question is not, is this activity a violation of copyright?—merely being in a position to ask that question would indicate that there is some level of evidence to indicate that the activity does violate copyright law. Instead, the question being asked should be, can a strong case be made that would indicate this activity is *not* a violation of copyright? If a strong argument can be developed indicating that a given activity does not violate copyright, and a judge agrees with the argument in court, then the legal precedent effectively excludes that particular activity from the law. Ultimately, this means that many activities that are not directly covered by copyright law or previously covered by legal precedent continue to act as legal gray areas, until tested in a court of law.

Currently copyright law taken as a whole "gives the owner of copyright the exclusive right to do and authorize others to do the following":

1. To reproduce the work in copies or phonorecords;
2. To prepare derivative works based upon the work;
3. To distribute copies or phonorecords of the work to the public by sale or other transfer of ownership, or by rental, lease, or lending;
4. To perform the work publicly, in the case of literary, musical, dramatic, and choreographic works, pantomimes, and motion pictures and other audiovisual works;
5. To display the work publicly, in the case of literary, musical, dramatic, and choreographic works, pantomimes, and pictorial, graphic, or sculptural works, including the individual images of a motion picture or other audiovisual work; and
6. In the case of sound recordings, to perform the work publicly by means of a digital audio transmission.[11]

Of these provisions, it should be somewhat obvious that the first and third are the ones that bear the most on online piracy—just ignore the obvious "digital audio" reference in the last provision for now. Making an unauthorized copy of a work, in any form, is a violation of copyright. This includes downloading a copyrighted work, making a copy of a file containing copyrighted work on a single computer, ripping content from a CD or DVD onto a computer, or even copying music from a computer to a portable device (such as an iPod)—all could be considered violations of the first provision. Based entirely on the letter of the law, merely opening a copyrighted file on a computer (which, at a technical level, creates a copy from the contents of the hard drive to memory) may actually be considered a violation of copyright as well. The third provision, protecting authors' rights to distribute copies of copyrighted works, extends to cover activities such as sharing and hosting. In any given file transfer, the person making the copyrighted file available for download, an activity commonly known as hosting, violates this provision by distributing the copy once requested by the downloader. If we again choose to follow the letter of the law, this could potentially include transferring a copyrighted file from one computer to another through a home network. However, there is an important, and hotly contested, distinction to be made here. Merely hosting, or making available, a copyrighted file online does not in itself constitute a violation of copyright law. As an example of legal precedent in action, this was recently made clear as courts barred the RIAA from using evidence that individuals have merely hosted copyrighted files on their computers as an indicator of unlawful distribution.[12]

Of the remaining provisions, two more somewhat clearly fail to directly concern forms of online piracy, given that public performance and display are generally not activities readily associated with P2P use or the warez scene. The sixth provision, while directly mentioning digital audio, was primarily designed to prevent Internet radio stations from publicly broadcasting songs without authorization—a process that, technically, is not covered by the first provision. But the remaining provision, which focuses on derivative works, does have something of a secondary impact on online piracy. The third provision basically provides authors the right to create derivative works—works that are similar to the original. For example, if I were to create and publish my very own Mickey Mouse cartoon, I would be in violation of copyright—only Disney has the right to create Mickey Mouse cartoons. This provision has a secondary impact on online piracy in the sense that having easy access to such a broad range of copyrighted digital materials makes the production and publication of derivative works much easier and more popular. One prominent example of an unauthorized derivative work intersecting with online piracy is the mashup artist Danger Mouse and the *Grey Album*. *Mashups* are musical works created entirely from segments of other songs, which are mashed together, usually using the vocal track from one song and the instrumental tracks from another. In 2004, musical artist Danger Mouse chose to combine the vocal tracks from rapper Jay-Z's *Black Album* and instrumental samples from the Beatles' *White Album* and released the resulting album in limited quantities. British music corporation EMI, who holds the copyrights to the Beatles' work, immediately took action to end the distribution of the album but, in the process, drew public attention to the existence of the album. P2P users quickly began sharing copies of the album through P2P networks, and the album became one of the most popular musical works of 2004. Based partially on the popularity of the *Grey Album*, P2P networks have continued to be used to distribute other forms of derivative works in violation of copyright, in addition to likely providing the source material.

These provisions are all the intellectual property industry needs to threaten individual P2P users with legal action. While the majority of the major industry associations have avoided doing so, one in particular has attempted to fully take advantage of its right to protect its intellectual property: the RIAA. The RIAA announced its intentions to begin suing P2P users on September 8, 2003.[13] Since that first round of lawsuits, the RIAA has continued to regularly target P2P users with legal action, resulting in an estimated 30,000 individuals who have fought their cases or settled out of court.[14] As described in Chapter 4, the RIAA has contracted with businesses that specialize in monitoring, tracking, and collecting digital evidence against infringing P2P users. While this evidence cannot definitively prove that a specific individual was behind the keyboard, sharing the files in question as the monitoring software attempted to download them, in a civil case, such a high level of proof is not necessary. The RIAA has demonstrated that judges in civil cases are sufficiently swayed merely by demonstrating that the IP address from which the file was being shared online is associated with an account holder name through the Internet service provider (ISP). In these cases, statutory damages are awarded to the copyright holder, ranging between $750 and $30,000 for each act of infringement, or each song or recording copied. These penalties were once smaller but were increased by the Digital Theft Deterrence and Copyright Damages Improvement Act of 1999. This can potentially result in extremely high fines for those found guilty of copyright violation. The majority of these cases are never actually entered into the legal system in any way and are instead settled out of court. From the perspective of the RIAA, these lawsuits have been extremely effective. As described in Chapter 5, surveys of Internet users seem to indicate that illegal P2P use has decreased in the wake of RIAA lawsuits. Those operating the systems that support P2P networks tell a different story, however. According to private P2P network researchers and usage statistics from popular BitTorrent sites, such as ThePirateBay.org, P2P use has been steadily on the rise following the initial announcement by the RIAA to sue P2P users. These seemingly conflicting reports, combined with the public backlash the RIAA has received for initiating the lawsuits, have generally prevented the other intellectual property industry associations from following too closely in the RIAA's footsteps. That doesn't necessarily imply that P2P users who download and share software and games are completely free of risk—at any time, the organizations that hold the rights to such media may change their minds and begin brandishing legal threats.

Further defining digital copyright law are the NET Act, the DMCA, and the PRO-IP Act, which primarily set criminal penalties for copyright infringement activities beyond certain monetary thresholds. The NET Act originally created criminal penalties for the digital reproduction or distribution of copyrighted works with a retail value totaling $1,000 or more within a 180-day period. If you recall from the previous chapter, assigning a dollar value to acts of online piracy can be difficult, but the law effectively assigns this duty to the victims of the case: the copyright holders. The penalties for distributing software totaling more than $1,000, as defined by the copyright holder, include the following[15]:

- A minimum of one year in prison and a fine for distributing between 1 and 9 copies of a copyrighted work totaling $2,499 or less
- A minimum of three years in prison and a fine for distributing more than 10 copies of a copyrighted work totaling $2,500 or more

The PRO-IP Act increases the criminal penalties set forth by the NET Act, allowing judges to sentence copyright infringers who distribute more than $2,500 to the extended period of jail time once given only to repeat offenders. Additionally, it broadens the types of material the government can seize from someone who is being tried for criminal copyright infringement, including anything that might have been used to facilitate the copying and distribution of the content in question. Again, these laws do not directly affect average P2P users—while it is certainly *possible* that a single P2P user could share $1,000 or $2,500 worth of content within a period of 180 days (particularly with a high-bandwidth connection), these laws were primarily designed to target the big fish in the warez scene and have been utilized accordingly. Even if a P2P user were to share such a large amount of content, which is not entirely uncommon, there exists no mechanism to actually gather evidence that an individual has shared a specific number of copies on most P2P networks.

Moving beyond even the actual copying and distribution of copyrighted content, the DMCA additionally attaches civil and criminal penalties to circumventing copyright protection measures put into place by copyright holders to make copying difficult or impossible. This means that under the DMCA, a single act of circumventing copyright protection measures allows the copyright holder to file a civil lawsuit against the individual who cracked the content. If the court finds that the circumvention was performed willfully and for financial gain, the act can potentially carry fines of up to $500,000, along with a prison sentence of up to 5 years for the first offense.[16] Like the NET Act, the DMCA has criminalized some fairly routine-seeming activities. Under the DMCA anticircumvention provision, making a single backup copy of a retail DVD, which is protected by a form of weak encryption, is technically a criminal act. In addition, the software (or any other circumvention device) that might allow someone to break the DVD encryption and create a copy is illegal to develop or distribute. Importantly, the DMCA also provides what are commonly known as safe harbor provisions, which specifically protect ISPs from liability when their users illegitimately transmit or make available copyrighted data via the Internet through their connections. As such, even when users of an Internet connection service illegally transmit or store copyrighted material through the systems owned by that service, the service providers themselves may not be held responsible for the copyright violation. However, on being notified using what is commonly known as a DMCA takedown notice by a copyright holder, the ISP is required to remove any potentially infringing content, until the poster can demonstrate that the content has been legally published online.

At this point, I imagine that you may be panicking, at least a little. Even if you don't use P2P programs, just playing a song on your computer might make you a pirate under current copyright law. With the balance of power shifted so far over to the intellectual property industry, the RIAA could be breaking down your door with a fist full of legal documents any second! Well, not so fast. There are segments of the law designed to protect consumers when they copy without permission under some specific circumstances. In copyright law, this is known as fair use. You probably have heard this phrase used to justify creating copies of content in one context or another. Many use fair use as a justification, but few actually know what is covered by fair use. Unfortunately, the fair use provisions in copyright are somewhat vague and in some ways potentially conflict with the DMCA. This makes actually attempting to use copyrighted material under fair use something of a scary proposition—it can be difficult to tell if you are operating in a legal gray area, just waiting for a court case to happen. Fair use outlines four legal criteria for determining if the use of a work falls under fair use:

1. The purpose and character of the use, including whether such use is of commercial nature or is for nonprofit educational purposes
2. The nature of the copyrighted work
3. Amount and substantiality of the portion used in relation to the copyrighted work as a whole
4. The effect of the use on the potential market for or value of the copyrighted work

Additionally, the law allows the creation of backup or archival copies of *software*. A case could be made to include media such as DVDs, which contain software of a sort, but the law does not cover downloaded copies of content already on your hard drive. These backup or archival copies can only be made when the following three conditions are met[17]:

1. The new copy is being made for archival (i.e., backup) purposes only
2. You are the legal owner of the copy
3. Any copy made for archival purposes is either destroyed or transferred with the original copy, once the original copy is sold, given away, or otherwise transferred

So you're on your own when it comes to determining if your potential violation of copyright is or is not qualifiable as fair use. There are no solid guidelines, until the judge makes a decision on the activity in question during a copyright case—remember what I said previously, that the real question is, can a strong case be made that would indicate this activity is *not* a violation of copyright? If you were panicked before, talking about the gray area of fair use probably has not helped all that much, particularly given that some of the laws are in contradiction to one another. If you make a backup copy of your software but need to break the copyright protection mechanism to do so, are you violating the DMCA? Before you light your computer on fire in an attempt to destroy the evidence, know this: as uncomfortable as it might be knowing that simply copying a song to your iPod violates copyright, the simple fact of the matter is that nobody will know but you. I'm not suggesting that that makes the way the law is structured acceptable for average consumers, but merely that the way the law is carried out locally is what matters most in many situations, and so long as the RIAA hasn't installed a camera behind your computer to watch you make copies, you should be just fine. Even if it has, pursuing such a case would not be in the interest of the RIAA. It seems unlikely that a judge would deem someone copying music he owns to a portable music player in violation of copyright, and making a decision on the side of the defendant would clearly establish such behavior as legal, thereby (slightly) shifting the overall balance of power back to the consumer. So the fair use gray area is something of a double-edged sword.

One final recent change in law has the potential to indirectly affect P2P users: the Higher Education Opportunity Act (HEOA) of 2008. Within this 1,158-page piece of legislation lie three new requirements for colleges and universities that concern illegal P2P use. These three requirements are an attempt to restrict and reduce illegal file sharing on college campuses by forcing college network administrators to take action. Specifically, the law requires colleges and universities to do the following:

1. [The development of] plans to effectively combat the unauthorized distribution of copyrighted material, including through the use of a variety of technology-based deterrents; and

2. To the extent practicable, offer alternatives to illegal downloading or peer-to-peer distribution of intellectual property, as determined by the institution in consultation with the chief technology officer or other designated officer of the institution.

3. [Communicate] institutional policies and sanctions related to copyright infringement [to students], including:

   a) an annual disclosure that explicitly informs students that unauthorized distribution of copyrighted material, including unauthorized peer-to-peer file sharing, may subject the students to civil and criminal liabilities;

   b) a summary of the penalties for violation of Federal copyright laws; and

   c) a description of the institution's policies with respect to unauthorized peer-to-peer file sharing, including disciplinary actions that are taken against students who engage in unauthorized distribution of copyrighted materials using the institution's information technology system (Article 493, Section 29)

The intellectual property industries, primarily the RIAA and MPAA, lobbied heavily for these regulations, despite the willingness of colleges and universities to work with these organizations. For this reason, college administrators are somewhat bitter about this law, feeling as if they were already doing enough work to prevent illegal P2P prior to the passage of the HEOA. Regardless of how college administrators feel about the law, however, they are expected to comply. This means that P2P users on college campuses can expect to see additional technical methods put into place for the management of P2P traffic. Perhaps even more important, however, is that the HEOA acts as a warning shot for college administrators, signaling that Congress is watching, as they attempt to reign in illegal file sharing. As such, it is likely that efforts taken by college administrators to do so will become increasingly public and restrictive, in an attempt to demonstrate to Congress that further legislation is not necessary, despite the words of industry lobbyists.

IS PIRACY THEFT?

No. The RIAA and MPAA have frequently described piracy in all forms as theft, but the law treats the two activities very differently. The most common advertisements by the MPAA have begun to appear on retail DVDs and in movie theaters: in one, viewers are asked if they would steal a DVD from a store, and then online piracy is portrayed as an equivalent crime. Somewhat ironically, the ad itself visibly demonstrates the difference between the two activities. When someone walks into a store and steals a DVD or CD, the store selling those products has one less to sell. When an Internet user makes a copy of digital content without authorization from the copyright holder, the copyright holder has lost nothing. In this way, digital content can be seen as a public good—when someone makes a copy, the original source remains intact. That does not mean, however, that someone can't make a copy and never pay for the content. Regarding the issue of lost sales, Lessig describes three different types of online pirate:

A) Those who download instead of purchasing
B) Those who download to sample content before they purchase it
C) Those who download to gain access to content no longer available in stores

To these three, I would add a fourth category:

D) Those who would never or could not have paid to gain access to the content[18]

Based on these categories, copyright holders only suffer a lost sale under type A piracy. In the remaining cases, copyright law is being violated, but in such a way that does not inflict any harm on the copyright holders. Indeed, it could be argued that type B piracy actually increases sales, as consumers find more music they enjoy through P2P networks. Unfortunately, there is no effective way to distinguish between these forms of piracy, and as such, any attempts to regulate each type of online piracy do so regardless of the harm to the copyright holder. There is something of an overlap between the legal definition of theft and the activity of online piracy—after all, something is being consumed without payment—but what matters more is how copyright law has separated the acts of making a copy of a work and the physical theft of a work. While the laws that make this distinction could be changed by Congress, it is unlikely that this will ever happen, given the long history of piracy in the United States.

SUMMARY

Overall, it is extremely unlikely that we will ever see the criminal prosecution of average P2P users. While there have been some law enforcement operations specifically targeting warez groups who use P2P for distribution, without persistent and expensive surveillance, it would be extremely difficult to gather enough evidence to successfully try a case against P2P users who just barely meet the conditions for criminal punishment. On the other hand, the RIAA and MPAA have continued to civilly sue individual P2P users on the basis of the significantly weaker evidence available to them. As such, there continues to be a level of legal risk endured by those who share copyrighted material online. Generally, if you decide to use P2P networks in violation of the law, following the steps outlined in Chapter 3 should reduce your risk at least slightly—even more so if you avoid sharing copyrighted materials and stick to downloading. Concerning those activities that were made illegal by the DMCA, as long as you aren't developing and distributing copyright protection circumvention tools, you will probably be just fine. While it may not be comfortable knowing that merely by copying the content of a legally purchased DVD movie to your hard drive, you are in violation of the law, it is unlikely that the movie industry will ever know, or particularly care, that you did so. This isn't to say that that makes the law as it is written OK, just that for most people, it is functionally irrelevant, regardless of the potential punishments.[19] Remember that the law as written can be interpreted in very different ways, depending on the situation—particularly in the realm of digital copyright.

Chapter 7

CASE STUDIES

While I've already covered the technical processes by which copyright holders go about identifying and suing P2P users and the legal mechanisms that allow them to do so, there's something to be said for taking a look at how those processes play out in real life. In this chapter, I'll provide a number of different examples of the ways in which copyright law has been enforced, including criminal cases, civil cases against P2P users, and civil cases against businesses. The first case, concerning criminal copyright violation, is drawn from experiences during a raid on the Rochester Institute of Technology (RIT) campus and information from reports of the operation as carried out by law enforcement. Then, I'll describe two cases in which individuals were accused of violating copyright through P2P networks by the Recording Industry Association of America (RIAA). I've chosen to focus on the RIAA because it has initiated legal action against more individuals than any other organization in history: over 30,000 P2P users across five years of near-continuous legal action.[1] Obviously, this pegs the RIAA as the main threat to those violating copyright over P2P networks. And given that music piracy appears to be the most prevalent form of online piracy, if you or someone you know is planning to use P2P networks for piracy, it is likely that music piracy, and therefore the RIAA, can potentially be involved. Additionally, the other arms of the intellectual property industry have either sued relatively few P2P users, such as the Motion Picture Association of America (MPAA), or have generally attempted other means to discourage copyright violation through P2P networks, such as the Business Software Alliance and the Entertainment Software Association (ESA). Each of these two cases, one typical and one unusual, can tell us something about how the process really works and about what it might be like to be targeted for legal action by a copyright holder. Finally, I'll provide information on the civil cases brought by the intellectual property industry against Napster and Grokster, two companies attempting to profit off of the P2P phenomenon.

CRIMINAL COPYRIGHT INFRINGEMENT (THE WAREZ SCENE): OPERATION BUCCANEER AND OPERATION BANDWIDTH

On the night of December 11, 2001, I stood in the middle of a cold Rochester, New York, parking lot, watching on as two friends frantically loaded their computers onto a covered pickup truck. Hours earlier, the U.S. Customs Agency and Federal Bureau of Investigation (FBI) had begun a raid on the RIT campus, part of an international effort known as Operation Buccaneer. My two friends, who had been running pirate servers of their own, were tipped off by other warez scene members a few hours following the initial raids. By tossing equipment into their cars, they were attempting to hide the evidence until the raid came to an end. Once they had finished loading up their equipment, they got into the car and began driving around Rochester—as if the law enforcement officers wouldn't wait for them if they were two of the students targeted. By that point, I had returned home and begun monitoring the raids on campus through an underground Web site that provided information on the groups being raided as the news traveled through the Internet Relay Chat (IRC) channels and communication networks of the warez scene. My friends drove through most of that night, hoping that there wouldn't be a group of officers waiting at their door when they returned. The underground Web site, operated by a member of the warez scene known only as "ttol," continued maintaining the site over a period of weeks, adding information about Operation Buccaneer as it progressed through 65 searches in the United States and five other countries.[2] The raids targeted members of some of the most prominent warez groups, including members of Drink or Die and Razor1911, both of which are still in operation even today. As it turned out, my friends were not actually being targeted by law enforcement officials, but both made a decision to keep a low network profile for a while, in fear that the RIT network might be under surveillance. Both were members of Razor1911, and an interview with one of them can be found in Appendix A. Following the raids, RIT network traffic dropped by 40 percent, as both the six servers taken by law enforcement and an unknown number of other pirate servers run by students were removed from the network. The amount of traffic continued to stay low for months, until students decided that the danger had passed and brought their servers back online one by one. Overall, Operation Buccaneer resulted in the conviction of 16 members of the warez scene, 13 of whom were given federal prison sentences of up to 46 months.[3]

Prior to the busts of 2001, federal agents had covertly spent considerable resources infiltrating the warez scene as part of an effort known as Operation Bandwidth. As part of a joint effort between the Department of Defense Criminal Investigative Service, (strangely) the Environmental Protection Agency (EPA) Office of the Inspector General, and the FBI, a false FTP site was created, hosted out of Las Vegas, Nevada, and known as Shatnet. The Shatnet FTP site was run for six months, from June to November 2001, and hosted a variety of programs, games, and movies uploaded by members of a warez group known as RogueWarriorz (RWZ).[4] IRC channels were used to invite members to the site, providing them with password-protected access. Once FBI special agent Ray Leber had gained the trust of RWZ, he offered members of the group 60-GB hard drives. Once the drives were accepted, Leber was provided with their home addresses for shipment, which were then used to raid the households of the RWZ members following the closing of Shatnet. Plainclothes law enforcement officers raided their homes, equipped with flak jackets and cameras, seizing all the computer equipment used by the RWZ members. Operation Bandwidth raids resulted in the prosecution of 21 RWZ members but additionally provided law enforcement with information on group members located at RIT. This information was eventually used during Operation Buccaneer, resulting in the raid on the RIT campus.

Worth a mention here is a description of online pirates who are actually prosecuted under criminal copyright law. Possibly because of the focus on warez groups, or to avoid being placed in an unpleasant political situation, federal law enforcement tends to prosecute primarily older pirates. The ages of those prosecuted using evidence gathered by Operation Bandwidth ranged from 21 to 52, with the majority of the RWZ members being in their thirties.[5] Many of the top members of the warez scene are not high school students or college undergraduates, but are actually older, working professionals. In the underground reports of the busts, information about the experiences of RWZ member "peaces" is provided, and "ttol" states that

> peaces was in Chicago. The local police tricked peaces into opening the door. They had some problems with peaces' son [recently] and asked her if she had anymore problems. She said no, and they asked if they could come in and talk to her. When she opened the door, all the agents came in.[6]

Like the majority of modern computer criminals, warez scene members frequently do not fit the common stereotype of the male, introverted, middle-class teenager surfing the Internet in a darkened room. "Peaces" was actually Suzanne Piece, a 38-year-old mother living in Lombard, Illinois. Many of these individuals are average people, with jobs, families, and homes.

The combined results of Operation Bandwidth and Operation Buccaneer should make evident the effort involved in gathering evidence for criminal copyright violation cases. Those who were raided and prosecuted were not individual P2P users, despite the fact that Napster, KaZaA, and Gnutella were already widely popular and being supplied in part through warez scene releases by late 2001. Instead, the operations focused solely on key members of many of the more prominent warez groups, who were seen by law enforcement to traffic in millions of dollars' worth of pirated content, well above that of the small-by-comparison $2,500 limit set by the NET Act. For the most part, little has changed since the busts of the late 1980s and 1990s in terms of the methods used to gather evidence against warez scene members. The technologies have changed and the laws have changed, but the warez scene itself has largely remained the same. Where there was once bulletin board systems and conference call lines, there are now FTP sites and IRC channels—but all can still be infiltrated by gaining the trust of scene members through the use of sting operations. Here, too, it is evident that like the procedures used by the intellectual property industry to gather evidence for civil cases, law enforcement targets those who distribute and/or host copyrighted works, although merely logging into an FTP site being run as a sting operation, such as Shatnet, is likely enough reason for law enforcement to investigate further. Simply put, these types of investigations are extremely costly, and as such, law enforcement seeks to maximize the results of such investigations. Faced with the decision to target either P2P users, who must be investigated on an individual basis and are unlikely to introduce new copyrighted content onto the network on their own, or the warez scene, which can be investigated in organized groups and initially supply a large percentage of the copyrighted content available on P2P networks, the choice is somewhat obvious. So, fear not, P2P users—the FBI (and yes, maybe even the EPA) are unlikely to be knocking (or breaking down) your door anytime soon. But, as you should already know by this point in the book, there *is* a possibility that you'll find a strange message in your e-mail inbox.

CIVIL COPYRIGHT VIOLATION (P2P USERS)

John: The Average Recording Industry Association of America (RIAA) Lawsuit

John[7] is a 21-year-old student attending a major engineering college in the Northeast and nearing the completion of his degree. I first met John as a student in one of the courses to which I was assigned as a teaching assistant, and he agreed to do an interview with me describing his experiences with the RIAA. Prior to attending college, he had become an Internet user sometime in the mid-1990s, along with many others of his generation. And as many others did, he started out on America Online (AOL), simply chatting and using the service's many features. At one point, a friend of his happened to point out that by choosing to access the right private chat rooms (a feature that allowed a user to specify the name of a chat room, allowing access only to those who knew the name of the room), he could download files being shared by others through server bots in the room. At the time, these files were primarily limited to software and images, given dial-up bandwidth constraints. John quickly learned how to use the bot system and was soon downloading software somewhat regularly. From there, he moved on to Napster, while it was still up and running. Once he began college classes, he began using other forms of P2P networks, including Gnutella and Fast-Track, guided primarily by online tutorials and a general knowledge of how the clients worked. Then he was introduced to BitTorrent by friends he met at college and began using it as his primary P2P network. Even though, at this point, he knew that he was violating copyright law, between his previous experience with other P2P programs and the perception that nearly everyone he knew was pirating music, movies, and software via P2P networks without negative repercussions, it just seemed like the thing to do. When asked how common P2P use was on his campus, he responded, "Oh, it's *very* common. I can't believe how common it is, it seems like everyone does it." Besides, "the record company and artists are already making millions . . . [the songs] were so readily available, it just seemed so convenient to do."

On average, he tended to download about two albums and three movies every week, sticking mainly to movies that had already come out on DVD. Specifically, John would use the campus Internet connection to download his files, always running the client software in the background while studying in the library or attending classes. He thought that the nature of BitTorrent transfers, which largely prevent any one person from sending the entire file being shared to any other single person, would protect him from any copyright disputes. Additionally, he was completely unaware that Internet protocol (IP) blacklisting software, such as PeerGuardian, even existed, so he was operating his client without any protection whatsoever. And while he generally ignored his sharing ratio on the torrents in which he participated, he made no attempt to restrict the amount he shared while he was downloading. Given the speed of the university Internet connection, it was likely that he shared quite a bit with others. Unaware that he had been found sharing music through BitTorrent by the RIAA (likely through MediaSentry), he left to study abroad in Australia. While there, he received an e-mail from the dean of students of his university, warning him that the RIAA had subpoenaed the school to gain access to information that would identify him for further legal action. He and 18 other students at the college had been targeted. Despite not knowing exactly what the RIAA was at the time, he had heard about other students being sued and prepared to receive additional information about the case. Rather than being sent the mountains of paperwork he expected would be involved in such a situation, he instead was sent an e-mail from the RIAA with a link to their somewhat amateur-looking settlement Web site. Rather than responding immediately, he hesitated. Partially, this was due to the strangeness of the e-mail and Web site: the way it was all being presented made John think that it might be some kind of Internet scam. However, another part of him wanted to ignore the problem, fearing it would potentially ruin his time in Australia.

Eventually, he received a call from his father back in the United States. He had received a package containing information about the suit in the mail. His father, too, was skeptical about the package, however, so once John returned home, they began researching what they were facing. Despite the seriousness of the situation, his family seemed only sympathetic to John's situation. When asked how his family reacted on learning of the suit, John responded, "They felt it was unfortunate that I got caught, but I don't think they were disappointed in me because they also benefited from it. I would make them CDs for Christmas and birthdays. My dad loved all the oldies [CDs] I would make for him." John began to learn more about the RIAA and the settlement process. He called a number listed on the settlement site, but the lawyers he contacted were of very little help, claiming that as mere representatives, they could not speak for the RIAA. This call would be the closest personal contact John would have with the RIAA throughout the settlement process. Back at the university, John's friends were all shocked that he had been targeted with a lawsuit. Some were surprised just to hear that the stories about the RIAA suing P2P users were actually true, let alone that someone they knew was being targeted. In the end, John decided to accept the settlement offer. Unfortunately, the RIAA settlement system is set up in such a way that it puts pressure on the person being targeted to make a decision quickly. As time passes following the initial offer, the amount the individual needs to pay increases. While John's initial settlement offer was the average $3,000, by the time he had decided to pay a few weeks later, he then owed $4,100. After paying the settlement—with a check by mail, just to be absolutely sure he had a record of the transaction if it turned out to be a scam—the RIAA demanded that John delete all of the files he had downloaded. Additionally, they warned him that they would pursue further legal action should he be found again on the P2P networks. Overall, using the settlement site, e-mail notifications, and the settlement offer, no information about John's behavior, or the threat of legal action, was ever actually entered into the legal system. Fearing that he was then added to some kind of pirate watch list, John has since refrained from using P2P networks but indicated that he has found other, "safer" ways to download his music.

With the exception of a few interesting snags, such as studying abroad and choosing to wait to settle, the case brought against John was a typical one. The RIAA subpoenas the Internet service provider, the defendant is notified about a settlement option, and then the defendant quickly accepts, fearing an extended and expensive court battle. That said, we can still learn quite a bit from John's experiences. For one, John's story shows us that the perception that "everyone is doing it" is still a pervasive one, and because "everyone is doing it," the sense among users is that it's OK to do. Regardless of how federal copyright law is written, and regardless of what the consequences for violating it might be, the *local* perception and practice of that law is what really matters. Once John started attending college, using P2P networks to download music and movies just seemed like the thing to do, and despite having someone so close to them become a target for legal action by the RIAA, everyone around John at his college is probably still doing the same thing. The same can be said for his family at home, who loved the CDs that John made for them as presents, rather than somehow rejecting the gifts and explaining that he was violating copyright. Everywhere John went, it was OK—even encouraged—to engage in online piracy, and to an extent, that made any potential legal consequences seem distant and vague. The fact of the matter is that few people really even know for sure what the law is or have actually read the law. What matters most is the everyday, local practices of the people around you, especially when the law is an inconvenience. However, "everyone else was doing it" doesn't make for a good defense when someone is actually found in violation of the law.

Another lesson we can take away from John's case is that the RIAA (or any other copyright holder) is not there to help defendants. If you are targeted for legal action because of online piracy, you are a defendant and will be treated as such by the groups hired by the RIAA to handle settlements and lawsuits. As John quickly found out, nearly every aspect of the RIAA settlement process is at least somewhat hostile and unfriendly to the P2P user being targeted. The initial contact is a single e-mail, the settlement Web page is somewhat unprofessional looking, the people working the contact telephone number are unable to provide very much information—overall, it seems that even once the individual receives the physical information package in the mail, information about what is happening and alternative options is so scarce that it's unsurprising that John and his family were concerned about being scammed. While this makes the RIAA out to be something of a villain, try to think of things from its perspective. Its take is that the people sharing and downloading music from P2P networks are thieves. Whether you agree with this perspective or not (I don't), why should the RIAA help individuals who they see as stealing their profits for their own gain? Of course, this has garnered the RIAA something of a negative reputation, but at least it's consistent with what it says about online music pirates.

The final lesson from John's case is to have a plan in advance. While the risk is still small, particularly if there really are 10 million other P2P users out there at any given moment, engaging in piracy over P2P networks is still risky. If you choose to share music with others online, make sure you know in advance what the potential consequences are and how you might handle them if you ever find yourself facing them. The way these types of settlements are structured, the RIAA wants you to quickly panic and agree to settling, without having time to consider the alternatives. So make a plan in advance. I know, it's inconvenient, it's a hassle—everything P2P networks are not—but better you take the time to consider what you would do now than find yourself targeted for legal action and being forced to consider your plan of action as the settlement amount increases with every lost day. If you're still not convinced, take a look at what might have happened to John if he had done some research ahead of time. Instead of trying to decide what the best course of action would be, he could have already known that the settlement option was best for him and chosen immediately to take the offer. Doing so would have saved him $1,000. Now, I'm not saying that taking the settlement offer is the best option—it might not be for you; rather, I'm just saying that you should know about the dangers associated with online piracy and what you might do if you're ever faced with them. Reading this book is (I hope) a good start. If you're interested in reading what else John had to say about his experiences, read the entire interview transcript in Appendix B; it contains more detail, and it's interesting to read the story as John tells it.

Tonya Andersen: Fighting the RIAA

While John's case was an example of the usual process for these types of events, not all the individuals the RIAA has chosen to sue have gone the same route. A few have chosen to stand their ground, ignore the settlement offer, and take the case to court, despite pressure from the intellectual property industry. One of the most prominent of these cases has been *Atlantic v. Andersen.* Tonya Andersen, then disabled and caring for an 8 year old daughter, was living in Oregon at the beginning of her case in 2005. The case began for Andersen in a similar way as it had for John: she received a letter notifying her that she had been found in violation of copyright law and could potentially owe the recording industry hundreds of thousands of dollars. Like John, she, too, initially thought that the letter was a scam, but she proceeded to call the number provided, just to be sure. Andersen was accused of having shared 1,046 gangster rap songs on KaZaA, a charge she denied, offering her computer over to the representative on the phone for further analysis. The settlement support center set up by the RIAA was, of course, uninterested in taking her computer and suggested that she take the settlement offer. Unfortunately, she could not afford the settlement payment on her income, so she began to seek legal advice. The first lawyer she contacted also suggested that she take the settlement offer and declare bankruptcy, indicating that it was the only way to deal with such cases.

Andersen felt that such action would be unfair, given that she had not actually committed the acts of piracy, and continued her search for legal help. Eventually, she found Lory Lybeck, who agreed to represent her in the coming federal lawsuit and responded to the settlement offer with a counterclaim against the music industry. As soon as word of the counterclaim went out, the lawyers representing the RIAA stepped up their efforts to construct a case against Andersen. Part of their efforts included what would become one of the most widely reported events in the history of the RIAA lawsuits, as they attempted to target and contact Andersen's daughter as a defendant in the case. At the time the infringing activities took place, Andersen's daughter was only seven years old, an age at which it was extremely unlikely that she was literate enough to type the name of the top rap artist into a search box, let alone set up a P2P program to distribute over 1,000 songs. While under copyright law, the RIAA could potentially sue for up to $750 per song, the tactics used by the industry seem to indicate that it does not wish to bring cases to court, but rather to bully those who ignore the settlement agreement into submission. In this case, the RIAA had little evidence tying Andersen to the sharing, and Andersen could provide evidence backing up her defense with a simple Google search. By searching for the username that the RIAA claimed was responsible for sharing the songs, Andersen found that it could be tied to an individual living over 200 miles away. Then, just as it seemed that Andersen could possibly win the case, the RIAA dropped it after a computer forensics expert found no evidence of P2P use on Andersen's computer. The RIAA uncharacteristically moved to dismiss the case "with prejudice," exonerating Andersen from all wrongdoing. While in some ways, she won the case, the proceedings left Andersen with thousands of dollars of unpaid legal fees—significantly more than the original settlement offer made by the RIAA.[8] Andersen was now left in a position similar to the one in which she had originally found herself, where she was being presented with a bill she could not possibly afford, except this time, she had been largely deemed innocent. So once again, she decided to fight and brought a lawsuit against the RIAA accusing them of fraud and extortion under the Racketeer Influenced and Corrupt Organizations Act (RICO) act, originally written to prosecute organized criminals. While Andersen eventually dropped these charges, she won her case, and the RIAA was ordered to pay her over $100,000 in legal fees in May 2008. Spokespersons from the RIAA have so far avoided commenting publicly on the case but have suggested that those in court battles tend to stretch the facts to better their position in response to the legal tactics used in the Andersen case.

Any effort to sue individual P2P users on such a wide scale must inevitably encounter some blunders, and the Andersen case was one of the RIAA's largest. Not only did the RIAA misidentify the person behind the keyboard who committed the infringing acts, but they additionally had the misfortune of choosing someone to target with whom the public could so easily sympathize. Of course, targeting Andersen's young daughter in a seemingly punitive way didn't help much either. Despite where you might stand on the ethics of online piracy or how you feel about the somewhat questionable actions taken by the RIAA, it was still well within its legal rights by initiating such a lawsuit. The fact remains that those engaged in sharing music, movies, and software online do so in violation of copyright laws, and those who hold the copyright to the materials being shared have the right to defend themselves and the property they manage.

Just as with John's story, we can learn a few things from Andersen's case. First, despite the fact that the lawyers representing the RIAA tend to treat those being targeted with a lawsuit with a level of hostility, there are people and organizations to which someone in Andersen's position can look for help. If you should find yourself in such a situation, one of the best places to start looking for help is the blog of lawyer and Electronic Frontier Foundation member Ray Beckerman. Beckerman, based in New York, has represented some defendants in RIAA cases but has generally spoken out against the RIAA legal tactics both through his Web site and through various speaking engagements. Included on this site is a list of lawyers in 32 states willing to represent individuals interested in taking their RIAA file sharing cases to court. If you cannot afford a lawyer, Beckerman suggests (again, not in the form of legal advice) that you attempt to band together with others targeted by the same organization and pool money together to find a lawyer who will take on all of the cases at once. Beckerman's site additionally provides information and updates on all the major file-sharing cases that have been brought to court, including all the court documents on the Andersen case.[9] For college students looking for more immediate legal advice, universities often retain a lawyer on staff to provide students with free assistance. If you are a college student and you receive a notice, check to see if free legal advice is made available by your university.

Second, if you are targeted with legal action and decide to take your case to court, begin assembling records that may be helpful to your defense. Get what information you can about your case from the organization bringing suit against you and use that information to demonstrate your case. In Andersen's case, no technical knowledge was necessary to begin this process. Merely by taking some of the information provided about the infringing activity—the username that was observed sharing the files—and performing a simple Google search, Andersen was able to use the RIAA's information in her defense. Because Internet users frequently use the same usernames across different Web sites and accounts, Andersen was able to gather information about the person who was more likely responsible for the sharing activity. Because of the reduced standard of proof in civil courts, while she could not definitively prove that it was the same person, by matching the username and types of music the individual enjoyed to the evidence provided by the RIAA, she provided enough evidence to defend her case well. This evidence-gathering information may go beyond a simple Web search, however. If you do use P2P programs, do they keep a log of your activity? Can you demonstrate that you did not have Internet access at the time of the infringing activity? Could there possibly have been someone else using your Internet access at the time of the infringing activity, which is a significant danger for those with open or unsecured wireless access points? Do anything you possibly can to build your defense, as fast as you can—oftentimes valid digital evidence is only available for a limited amount of time.

Finally, Andersen's case indicates that there is hope for those who find themselves wrongfully (or even not so wrongfully) accused of illegal file sharing. One of the reasons so few of the cases brought by the intellectual property industry against individual file sharers has gone to court is simply because it often costs more to fight a long, drawn-out legal battle than it does to admit to the infringing activity and pay the settlement costs. By winning her case and being compensated for over $100,000 in legal fees through her subsequent lawsuit against the RIAA, Andersen has demonstrated that it is possible to defeat the standard evidence presented by the intellectual property industries in such cases. Admittedly, Andersen's case was a somewhat special one given her financial status, the exceedingly rough treatment she received from the RIAA, and strong corroborating evidence, all factors that likely swayed the judges' decisions. While not all cases will be so easily won, doing so is not impossible. Recently, other cases have demonstrated this as well, with a handful of other defendants since 2003 having successfully won their own cases. Keep in mind, however, that the RIAA has also won a number of the cases brought to court, extracting hundreds of thousands of dollars in fines from individual file sharers.

CIVIL COPYRIGHT INFRINGEMENT
(CORPORATIONS)

Many of the earlier P2P file-sharing networks utilized the hybrid P2P model, which, while making P2P communication simpler to implement, also created centralized points of failure that could be used to shut down the network. At the time these networks were being developed, facilitating digital piracy was something of a legal gray area, and many developers were creating advertising-based business models around P2P networks. Because having a centralized server was not yet seen as a legal problem, and because having a central server allowed companies to profit by advertising to peers, the hybrid model was actually the preferable solution. As such, a number of early developers maintained control over all the servers that allowed the network to run, forming companies around the new P2P networks in an attempt to profit from a user base numbering in the millions. The most prominent example of a company that adopted this model is, of course, Napster. For many early P2P developers, it was unlikely that the concept of being shut down by the intellectual property industry was ever a major consideration during the design process. Many were college students or recent graduates, and in the early 2000s, public conceptions of digital copyright were even fuzzier than they are today. After all, the servers being run by the P2P businesses were not actually *hosting* any copyrighted files, just indexing them and selling advertisements. Theoretically, this meant that the companies themselves were not actually violating copyright. Instead, they were providing a service that was merely a tool for sharing files between individual users, and any use of that service for copyright violation was entirely based on the actions of those users. Unfortunately, the RIAA did not see things in the same light Napster did, and the hybrid model provided a perfect target for litigation by copyright holders.

While Napster was developed by a college student, Shaun Fanning, the business itself was being run by Fanning's uncle, John Fanning. John Fanning claimed that he had read through a vast number of historical copyright cases and had determined that based on the argument that Napster was merely a tool that could be used for a variety of legitimate purposes, combined with portraying the copyright violation that was occurring through Napster as fair use, Napster had a 90 percent chance of winning any court battle.[10] On October 2, 2000, that prediction was put to the test, as the RIAA brought suit against Napster in *A&M Records v. Napster.* The plaintiffs in this case argued that Napster was guilty of secondary copyright infringement, a concept developed through legal precedent in the courts. There are two types of secondary copyright infringement, contributory and vicarious, both of which Napster was accused of. *Contributory infringement* occurs when a defendant knowingly contributes to infringing activities, whereas *vicarious infringement* occurs when a defendant can control or prevent the actions of the infringer and also knowingly profits from the infringement. The Napster operation seemingly fit all these requirements, given that it was knowingly developed for the explicit purpose of copyright infringement, it could theoretically attempt to filter copyrighted files from the network, and it was profiting from advertisements. The argument against Napster, the RIAA maintained, was not against P2P itself, but against the infringing use of P2P. The Napster defense lawyers argued back, accusing the RIAA of attempting to bring down Napster merely to maintain control over the production and distribution of music. They claimed that Napster use for infringing purposes fell under fair use and that doing so was no different than recording television or radio broadcasts.

On February 2, 2001, Judge Mary M. Schroeder declared that Napster could be held liable for both contributory and vicarious copyright infringement, upholding the ruling from the original suit brought against Napster by the RIAA in a lower court. The fact that search results were provided by centrally managed servers provided additional leverage for the intellectual property industry. In addition to substantial fines, Napster was ordered to begin filtering all copyrighted files from its network, a task the infrastructure was—theoretically—suited to perform. Because copyrighted works could potentially be filtered from the search results, the RIAA had Napster shut down until it could demonstrate that copyrighted files would no longer appear in Napster searches. While it makes sense that copyrighted works could be filtered from the Napster network with a simple list from the RIAA, in practice, such a task is nearly impossible. With varying file names and compression schemes, the same song can be represented by an infinite number of forms. Additionally, without copyrighted material, the Napster network would become far less popular, which in itself is enough to kill a P2P network. While Napster made a number of attempts to filter the network, watching on as their user base steadily fell, ultimately, they were forced to shut down the network. In July 2001, the network was officially disconnected, displacing millions of users to other, less centralized P2P services. Napster as it was originally conceived was gone, but the brand went on to support a subscription-based music service, which allowed users to download music protected by a digital rights management system for a monthly fee.

Despite the ruling, other enterprising coders and businesspeople continued to make attempts at forming a profitable business around the P2P phenomenon. Four years after the Napster decision, on March 29, 2005, a U.S. Supreme Court case was brought against Grokster and Streamcast (companies that developed the popular FastTrack network clients Grokster and Morpheus) by the MPAA. Rather than developing and managing an entire network, these companies simply developed client software for an existing network, placing advertisements in the interface to make the venture profitable. Prior to arriving at the Supreme Court, Grokster and Streamcast had won against MGM twice in the lesser courts, with each case being dismissed on the grounds of the *Sony Corp v. Universal City Studios* case of 1984. This landmark case protected Sony, who was then a VCR manufacturer, from liability when VCR users copied films in violation of copyright. The decision in the *Sony v. Universal* case was heavily criticized by the movie industry, and the Grokster case seemed to provide an opportunity to have the decision overthrown. Ultimately, the U.S. Supreme Court decided that Grokster and Streamcast were liable for secondary copyright infringement, just as Napster had been. However, the Court declined to overthrow the *Sony v. Universal* decision, emphasizing that a company must profit off the infringing activity to be held liable. In a sense, this decision prevents file-sharing services from profiting from wide-scale infringement of copyright, while at the same time maintaining the ability for nonprofit P2P networks to operate, regardless of the content being distributed.

Following the ruling, Grokster has closed its doors, and the software client it once provided is no longer distributed. Now, on visiting the Grokster site, Web users are confronted with an imposing message from the intellectual property industry:

The United States Supreme Court unanimously confirmed that using this service to trade copyrighted material is illegal. Copying copyrighted motion picture and music files using unauthorized peer-to-peer services is illegal and is prosecuted by copyright owners.

There are legal services for downloading music and movies.

This service is not one of them.

YOUR IP ADDRESS IS 24.***.***.*** AND HAS BEEN LOGGED.

Don't think you can't get caught. You are not anonymous.

This message describes the illegality of using P2P services to trade copyrighted material, while demonstrating that your (nonunique) IP address was logged, as if visiting the site was somehow in violation of the law. For those of you who are in some way considering creating a business based off illegal P2P use, don't. You will quickly find yourself in the shoes of Napster and Grokster, standing before a judge unconvinced by your fair use arguments.

SUMMARY

The world of digital copyright is a strange and complicated one, and one in which the balance of power has been increasingly pushed toward the interests of the intellectual property industry. This has been made apparent over the past decade, as legislators, law enforcement officials, the intellectual property industry, and the courts have determined how to handle the problem of online piracy. If you find yourself in the sights of the intellectual property industry for sharing copyrighted materials via P2P networks, the odds are undoubtedly stacked against you, regardless of your actual involvement in the activity itself. Whether the RIAA intends them to be so or not, active defense of these types of lawsuits are prohibitively expensive and must be conducted in the face of extremely hostile industry representatives. That said, there are people willing to help defend against these types of cases, and slowly, more RIAA cases are being successfully defended in court. Regardless of whether you ever find yourself a defendant in one of these cases, be sure to have a plan of action and know what you will do ahead of time, particularly if you are an active P2P user. While the risks are small, being prepared can make what is frequently a panicked, difficult decision into a more thought-out and rational one.

Chapter 8

THE FUTURE OF FILE SHARING

As we've seen throughout the preceding chapters, the world of online piracy and digital copyright is a turbulent one, with each successive generation of copying and distribution technologies creating new challenges for copyright holders and legislators. Each of these successive challenges bears a kind of family resemblance to its predecessors, as individual consumers begin to adopt and utilize these new technologies in ways that frequently infringe on copyright. What is next for online piracy, P2P, and the intellectual property industry? In this chapter, I'll describe some of the more recent developments in technology, law, and business that will come to bear on online piracy. I'll also briefly take on the role of the futurist and attempt to make some of my own predictions on what the future holds for the various stakeholders that populate the world of online piracy.

TECHNOLOGY

Industry/Antipiracy

While direct regulation through government legislation poses a clear threat to online piracy, indirect regulation through changes in technology may represent a far larger threat. The successful implementation of a P2P network relies heavily on a critical mass of average, nontechnical users. Napster, and the P2P networks that followed in its footsteps, brought digital piracy, which was once the exclusive domain of the technical elite, to a broader audience by making it convenient and simple. To truly make an impact on the prevalence of infringing P2P use, one need only make it inconvenient. Right now, this is precisely the tactic being used by Internet service providers (ISPs) and copyright holders, which, in some cases, have actually joined together under the same organization.[1] ISPs, the intellectual property industry, and device manufacturers are working in concert to increasingly lock down the spaces in which media are shared and consumed. As copyright scholar Lawrence Lessig notes in his book *Free Culture*, "they are succeeding in their plan to remake the Internet before the Internet remakes them."[2]

ISPs have already begun this process using a number of strategies, as I discussed in Chapter 3. Currently traffic shaping, which slows down specific types of network traffic (such as P2P) and speeds up others (such as e-mail), and bandwidth capping, which sets limits on the amounts individual users can upload and download, are the most common techniques used by ISPs to manage P2P use. These techniques do not distinguish between the use of P2P for legal and infringing purposes, making the legitimate use of P2P more difficult. However, these techniques represent only the beginning of attempts to manage of online piracy by ISPs. An entire industry has quietly sprung up around the development of online piracy management technologies, specifically constructed to fit the needs of both ISPs and, of course, universities. One such technology is being managed through a partnership between Kevin Bermeister, who once held a top position at the company that developed KaZaA, and Michael Speck, who once ran the enforcement division of the Australian equivalent of the Recording Industry Association of America (RIAA). This technology, announced in 2008, will supposedly replace all infringing P2P search results with links to legal online storefronts, forcing P2P users to purchase the content through the ISP, rather than downloading it illegally.[3] Other similar products are constantly being developed, as technologists sense the opportunities that lie within the uneasiness of ISPs and universities over online piracy. So far, public and government reactions to the more extreme forms of traffic shaping have been highly negative in the United States, as exemplified by the Federal Communications Commission ruling against ISP Comcast (which actively throttled BitTorrent traffic on its network). The more subtle forms of this type of regulation have generally been accepted by the majority of Internet users, primarily because when they are quietly implemented, relatively few users notice the changes. Even further locking down the ways in which we might be able to use P2P networks, and the content available through them, are the device manufacturers. Increasingly, companies that develop the hardware and software that allow Internet users to download, store, and consume the content available on the Internet are developing products that prevent piracy. This includes televisions, computers, operating systems, portable media devices, gaming consoles, and DVD players, among other devices. The companies that design and manufacture these devices are building in systems that verify the source of digital content and will only operate with content deemed legitimate. These systems are known by the industry as digital rights management (DRM)[4] and are specifically protected under the DMCA as copyright protection technologies. As these systems become integrated into the technologies that allow us to produce and consume media, the potential exists for piracy to once again become the exclusive province of the technical elite—those who have the expertise to circumvent strong DRM mechanisms.

In this way, piracy can be seen to be driving the development of an increasingly restrictive technological infrastructure. Then again, maybe *driving* is too harsh of a term to describe the effects of piracy on infrastructure. In the last chapter, I mentioned that the defense lawyers in the Napster case argued that the intellectual property industry was attempting to maintain control over the systems that allow for the consumption, creation, and distribution of media. While Napster lost its case, there was certainly something to be said for the argument itself. Control over these technologies, and therefore the media that are created and consumed through them, is highly profitable. As the level of control increases, the ability to force individuals to pay for the use or consumption of copyrighted media also increases. For example, imagine being asked to pay a licensing fee every time you post a video of yourself to the Internet with the radio playing (copyrighted music) in the background or being prevented from recording your favorite television show, forcing you to purchase copies in the store. Neither example is all that far off from being reality, and in both cases, the intellectual property industry has in some way mobilized the discourse of piracy in attempts to reign in these activities. When looked at from this angle, the specter of piracy becomes less of a reason for the development of restrictive media technologies and more of a convenient excuse. This is not to say that the intellectual property industry is composed entirely of evil masterminds, attempting to completely wrest control over digital content away from individuals, but it *is* an industry looking to maximize profit. All ethical issues aside, from the perspective of a profitable business, restricting media technologies makes sense in the short term, even while it may not be the most beneficial path for consumers.

Consumers/Anti-anti-P2P

From FTP to BitTorrent, new technologies that facilitate the copying and distribution of digital content have developed alongside computer and Internet technologies. Through the progression of these technologies, developers have attempted to increase the anonymity and security of file-sharing technologies, particularly as law enforcement and copyright holders have focused their attention on digital copyright violation. Each new form of restriction developed by ISPs, media device manufacturers, and the intellectual property industry is treated as a challenge to many open source developers, hobbyists, scholars, and crackers (who I will lump together simply as hackers for now[5]). Hackers represent a constant effort at attempting to liberate various forms of media from control—some do so to allow for fair use, some to knowingly violate copyright law, and some simply for the fun of it. This effectively results in an arms race type of scenario, with the intellectual property industry developing new methods of protection and control, while the hackers attempt to break them in record time. Only recently, the copyright protection measures developed for new high-definition Blu-ray Discs, initially expected to remain unbroken for 10 years, were cracked by open source hackers after a matter of months.[6] Competition between ISPs and device manufacturers, on one side, and hackers, on the other, has resulted in thousands of new copyright protection circumvention tools, P2P clients, and P2P networks.

Of the technologies developed by hackers and released for free on the Internet, those which most directly affect online piracy are the new forms of P2P networks. New efforts have been made to further anonymize and secure P2P networks to avoid identification by copyright holders. P2P networks that have support for anonymization and encryption are known as third-generation networks (hybrid P2P networks and true P2P networks were the first and second generations, respectively). As we discussed in Chapter 3, each computer on the Internet is assigned an Internet protocol (IP) address, allowing it to send and receive transmissions from other computers on the network. This address can be used by copyright holders and law enforcement to identify P2P users. One way in which third-generation P2P networks mask the IP address is by transferring all files through a proxy. In P2P networks, this simply means that all traffic on the network is transferred through a third node, rather than directly between the sender and receiver. As an example, say we had Ann and Bob, who are using a P2P network and want to send a file to one another. In most P2P networks, Ann would ask Bob for a file, and Bob would send it back to Ann. In a P2P network which communicates through a proxy, Ann would ask Bob for a file, and Bob would send the file to Carl, a third P2P user, who then sends the file through to Ann. This way, if Ann is actually collecting IP addresses for MediaSentry, she can never know who was originally sharing the file she tried to download. In addition to proxy methods, third-generation P2P networks encrypt the traffic between nodes. Encryption prevents those outside the network from monitoring, or listening in on, the traffic between nodes—as researchers Oberholzer-Gee and Strumpf did (see Chapter 5). First, this prevents any attempts to gather evidence against P2P users by monitoring their traffic, which, from a legal standpoint, is difficult at best. More important, encryption makes it difficult to block or filter P2P traffic at the ISP level. To those attempting to monitor and block only P2P, encrypted traffic could be absolutely anything. Of course, the large volume and pattern of traffic is usually an indicator of P2P use, even if one can't actually see what is being transmitted. One of the most common examples of third-generation P2P networks, utilizing both proxy methods and encryption, is the ANts network, an open source project started in 2004 by an Internet Relay Chat (IRC) user known as "Gwren." As a third-generation P2P network, ANts uses both encryption and proxy methods to protect its users.

The ANts network is essentially a more secure version of the Gnutella network—but by making radical changes to the typical P2P model, one developer believed he could exploit copyright law and make all file transfers, regardless of content, legal. This network is known as the Owner Free File System, or simply OFF. From the beginning of its development, OFF was designed specifically to challenge the ways in which copyright holders collect evidence against P2P users. In a somewhat ironically copyrighted open letter to the "Copyright Industry Associations of America," a programmer referring to himself as "The Digital Douwd" announced the initial release of OFF and warned the intellectual property industry of its own demise on August 14, 2006.[7] Years later, the industry has yet to fall, and OFF has failed to attract a significantly large user base, but the concepts behind OFF still have something to say about the direction in which P2P networks may be headed. The ways in which OFF operates are somewhat conceptually complex, exploiting the digital representation of content to push the boundaries of copyright law. Essentially, all digital content is a long string of numbers—hence the term *digital*. To an extent, the court has already demonstrated that sharing the strings of numbers that represent copyrighted works online is a violation of copyright law. Realizing this, OFF takes digital content and performs various mathematical operations on it—treating files as just really long numbers. By performing these operations, the copyrighted string of numbers representing a song or movie is converted to an entirely different, uncopyrighted string of numbers, which can then (theoretically) be legally shared and copied. Once the new string of numbers has reached its destination, the software then converts it back into the original format.[8]

Unfortunately, while the hacker community has excelled at developing technologies that circumvent the protections and barriers that hamper P2P use at a technical level, they are not traditionally well known for making the tools that do so accessible to a broader, nontechnical audience. Further hampering the third-generation P2P networks is the additional overhead required to transfer files. For each mechanism used to further anonymize and secure P2P traffic, more bandwidth, time, and processing power are required, all of which may slow the transfer of a file significantly. So while new P2P technologies have been developed that provide users with higher levels of anonymity, or that attempt to further muddy the waters of digital copyright law, these technologies have not yet been widely adopted. Simply put, they are inconvenient for the majority of P2P users. Without the numbers of average, less technically inclined users, these networks are not truly successful. As a result, because they are not successful, the measures used by the developers to make them more RIAA-proof have not been tested in courts. In the case of networks such as OFF, this means that they will perpetually exist in the fuzzy, legal gray area of technologies that have not yet been made legal through court rulings—in effect, allowing the challenge made by "The Digital Dowd" to go unanswered. For now, the third generation of P2P networks remains somewhat obscure, but it is very possible that these forms of networks may represent the future of online piracy, particularly as bandwidth and computing resources become increasingly inexpensive and widespread.

That does not mean, however, that hackers are not currently working on technologies that cause trouble for copyright holders and law enforcement attempting to gather evidence on P2P users. Rather than developing entirely new P2P networks, many are attempting to further secure the ones that are currently popular. The majority of these new technologies have been developed for the BitTorrent network, which has long been one of the favored methods of P2P file transfer for the more technically inclined. Most come in the form of encryption modules for existing BitTorrent clients, allowing third-generation P2P security over BitTorrent. More effective, however, are the changes being made by those who manage the sites that facilitate BitTorrent file sharing. One of the most popular BitTorrent trackers on the Web, ThePirateBay.org, has begun injecting random IP addresses into torrent swarms. This means that when MediaSentry checks to see which IP addresses are engaged in downloading and sharing any given file being monitored by BitTorrent, it cannot distinguish the real addresses of Internet users who are currently participating and the random addresses generated by the system.[9] While this tactic increases the number of individuals who are wrongly accused of online piracy, it makes it significantly more difficult for organizations such as the RIAA to claim that their evidence is valid in court, and it simultaneously results in numerous negative publicity incidents, as innocent individuals are brought to court. Furthermore, the users who are actually engaged in transferring files between each other do not need to take any action to allow this form of protection to work—sharing and downloading continues as normal. Undoubtedly, this type of tracker protection will spread from Pirate Bay to other BitTorrent sites, making accurate identification of BitTorrent users increasingly difficult for copyright holders.

Finally, a small group of startup businesses have recently appeared online, offering proxy and encryption services to Internet users for a monthly fee. Using a software client, paid users may either encrypt all their Internet traffic, route all their traffic through an anonymous proxy, or both. Regardless of whether they are Web surfing, writing e-mail, or sharing files on a P2P network, all traffic appears to be coming from the IP address of the proxy computer, rather than the users' own. Additionally, because the traffic between the user and the proxy computer is encrypted, it can be difficult for ISPs to identify, throttle, or block P2P file transfers. As these practices are becoming increasingly commonplace for ISPs, the services offered by these new businesses become more attractive to heavy P2P users. Incidentally, one of the largest of these services—known as Relakks—was developed by the same group of hackers who manage ThePirateBay.org. Located in Sweden, the service claims to maintain no records that would link a user to any specific time or Internet traffic and suggests that to actively monitor any Internet traffic running through its service, Swedish law enforcement officers would need to demonstrate that the offense being investigated carries a penalty of two or more years in prison.[10] For an American P2P user subscribed to the service, it is highly unlikely that either Swedish law enforcement or the intellectual property industry would manage to come close to gathering enough evidence to bring a copyright case to court.

Despite these developments by hackers, the battle for control of technology is still largely dominated by the ISPs and device manufacturers. The third generation of P2P networks is still missing its most important feature: users. Attempts to secure existing P2P networks are useful but not entirely effective, and few other than the extremely paranoid are willing to pay for encryption and proxy services. In addition, ISPs and device manufacturers effectively control the architecture on which all these activities take place. While rapid changes that restrict the range of action one can take online are both technically and socially implausible, the slow, incremental changes being made by these industries in that direction are very real and have gone largely ignored by the general public. As such, I imagine we can expect more and stronger restrictions on what consumers can and cannot do with the media equipment they purchase and the services to which they subscribe, a process that will make online piracy and P2P use increasingly difficult.

COPYRIGHT LAW

With the passage of the Prioritizing Resources and Organization for Intellectual Property (PRO-IP) Act so near a major economic crisis, it seems somewhat doubtful that additional copyright legislation is at the top of the agenda in Congress, or will be in the near future. Anything that might have had a significant impact on P2P users was largely stripped from PRO-IP, thanks in part to lobbying efforts by organizations such as the Electronic Frontier Foundation, signaling that Congress is finished with the issue for the time being. Furthermore, following the widespread adoption of Napster in 2000, there have been annual congressional hearings on P2P file sharing; 2008 was the first year in which there was no such hearing.[11] But while Congress seems to have finished with online piracy issues (at least temporarily), there are still a number of civil lawsuits against file sharers being played out in the courts. As I mentioned in Chapter 6, each of these cases will help to further define digital copyright law through precedent, each strengthening or weakening particular arguments used by both the plaintiffs and defendants in future cases.

Slowly, the courts are beginning to question the evidence being presented to them in the cases brought to them by the RIAA. The standards of proof are certainly lower for civil lawsuits, and the RIAA has used this to its advantage. In the *Arista v. Does* 1–17 case, which targeted students attending Oregon State University accused of infringing P2P use, as usual, the RIAA filed a suit against a group of unidentified students, then subpoenaed the ISP that owned the IP addresses from which the infringing activity originated—in this case, Oregon State University. Specifically, the university was asked to provide evidence linking these IP addresses to individual users. At this point, the broad majority of universities simply determine which user was using the IP address at the time of infringement and pass the information along to the RIAA, after sending a notice to the user being targeted. In this case, Oregon State University decided to make a motion to quash the subpoena, both on the grounds that doing so would place undue burden on them and that the RIAA had employed an organization—MediaSentry—that violated the privacy of their students under Oregon state law. The argument for the first claim struck at the weakness in the evidence used by the RIAA against P2P users: it is nearly impossible to determine who was actually behind the keyboard at the time of infringement, without finding a witness to the infringing activity. While the court seemed to have based its decision largely on the first claim, the Oregon Attorney General's Office additionally demonstrated that because MediaSentry had failed to register as a private investigator in the state of Oregon, in gathering evidence against the students, MediaSentry had violated their privacy, rendering the evidence invalid in court.[12] The court ultimately decided in October 2008 to grant Oregon State University's motion to quash the subpoena, and the case went no further. However, this sets the stage for other universities and ISPs to do the same when presented with subpoenas from the intellectual property industry.

Beyond the evidence presented to them, the courts are additionally beginning to question the damages awarded to copyright holders in such cases. These damages are frequently very high, as the statutory damages awarded can range between $750 and $30,000 per recording. According to this range of damages, an individual found liable for sharing a single, 15-track album could potentially be fined up to $450,000. Obviously, $450,000 is far, far more than one might pay in a store for the same album and is therefore much higher than the amount lost from the lost sale felt by the recording industry. The law is intended to penalize individuals who violate copyright, but when it was originally written, the law focused on those attempting to profit from the sale of illegitimate copies, not on file sharers. The NET Act changed that, but not the damages assigned to those found liable of copyright violation. Increasingly, courts are finding that the damages are extremely disproportionate to the harms experienced by copyright holders in file-sharing cases. Recently, in the *Capitol v. Thomas* case, Judge Michael Davis made the following comment:

> The Court would be remiss if it did not take this opportunity to implore Congress to amend the Copyright Act to address liability and damages in peer-to-peer network cases such as the one currently before this Court. . . . While the Court does not discount Plaintiffs' claim that, cumulatively, illegal downloading has far-reaching effects on their businesses, the damages awarded in this case are wholly disproportionate to the damages suffered by Plaintiffs. Thomas allegedly infringed on the copyrights of 24 songs—the equivalent of approximately three CDs, costing less than $54, and yet the total damages awarded is $222,000 . . . more than four thousand times the cost of three CDs.[13]

As with any other action that might make online piracy even marginally more attractive to Internet users, the RIAA and Motion Picture Association of America are strongly against reducing the damages assigned to those found liable for infringement. Given the strength of the entertainment lobby in government, it is fairly unlikely that Congress will adopt such changes to copyright law anytime soon. However, there is at least some potential for change, given the increasing number of judges taking issue with the RIAA cases and the excessive amounts of damages that individual P2P users are forced to pay. These damages are so large that one law professor is attempting to use one of the RIAA cases to demonstrate that they are actually unconstitutional. In *Sony v. Tenenbaum,* defendant Joel Tenenbaum chose to decline the settlement offer and bring the case to court, with the assistance of his mother, who is "a leading copyright and Internet lawyer," and an entire class of Harvard cyberlaw students.[14] The professor of the cyberlaw class, Charles Neeson, assisted Tenenbaum in filing a countersuit against the RIAA, claiming that the law being used by the RIAA against P2P users—the Digital Theft Deterrence and Copyright Damages Improvement Act of 1999—is actually a criminal statute, punishing violators with excessive penalties. By this logic, Neeson claims that the law is actually unconstitutional, violating both the Fifth and Eighth Amendments. If Neeson's argument is accepted by the courts, it may potentially end RIAA litigation, until a new statute is passed by Congress.[15]

In the legal realm, it seems that the arguments on which the RIAA and other intellectual property organizations rely to punish infringing P2P users are slowly being picked apart. For years, the RIAA has relied on a general lack of technical knowledge among P2P users and a strong adherence to copyright protection of traditional media to quickly win its cases, but as the public has generally become more informed about computer and Internet technologies, this has become increasingly difficult. Additionally, the RIAA has made quite a few enemies in the process of suing or settling with over 30,000 individuals using somewhat questionable legal evidence and lobbying for strengthened regulations from Congress. This includes a large cohort of legal scholars and university officials, in addition to many of the law and technology students currently working toward their degrees. While not all intellectual property organizations have engaged in suing individuals, the seemingly excessive actions of the RIAA have put these types of court cases in something of a negative light. Overall, it is somewhat surprising that the RIAA managed to get as far as it did using the evidence gathered by MediaSentry—but now it seems it may only be a matter of time before courts are no longer quite so sympathetic to its claims. While all of this appears on the surface to give P2P users the edge, this advantage may only last for a short time. The power of the entertainment lobby should not be underestimated, and if courts increasingly rule against copyright holders, there will likely be a large push to craft new copyright legislation.

BUSINESS

In addition to the recent technical and legal changes that are reshaping cyberspace and digital copyright, there have been some important developments in the business world concerning online piracy. These developments have somewhat secondary effects on online piracy, and in a way, they represent the institutionalization of what has commonly been the domain of the computer underground. Despite the epic struggle between the intellectual property industry and online pirates and hackers, there have been some attempts to reconcile the differences between the two groups to profit from the popularity of digital content, embracing P2P technologies, rather than fighting them. By far, the largest of these has been started by the developer of BitTorrent. The original developer of BitTorrent, Bram Cohen, formed a company named (obviously) BitTorrent, which is attempting to use BitTorrent technology to quickly and efficiently distribute entertainment. This may sound somewhat similar to the stories of Napster and Grokster, but Cohen's business differs in a number of significant ways. First, Cohen developed the BitTorrent technology and then released it to the public for free and never attempted to profit off the illegal distribution of copyrighted material, for which it became known. Second, BitTorrent actually represents an important innovation in online distribution, which has a wide variety of potential uses, as I explained in Chapter 3. Finally, Cohen and BitTorrent management actively attempted to partner with the intellectual property industry and device manufacturers after BitTorrent had proven itself as a robust tool through heavy use by Internet users. Because Cohen had neither engaged in nor facilitated any form of on-line copyright violation with BitTorrent—despite the fact that it is used by millions of other users to do exactly that—Cohen was well positioned to attract large content producers and device manufacturers. Currently Cohen licenses BitTorrent technologies to companies that are looking for an effective method of distributing media online, in addition to hosting the BitTorrent Entertainment Network, which provides users with both free and paid media downloads. So far, BitTorrent has formed partnerships with over 20 major content producers and device manufacturers, including 20th Century Fox, MGM, Paramount, Warner Bros., MTV, Netgear, and Dlink.[16] Through these partnerships, BitTorrent (the company) now holds enough influence to fight against attempts by ISPs to throttle or block P2P networking. This became particularly apparent as ISP Comcast secretly at-tempted to sabotage all BitTorrent connections, leading BitTorrent to play a role in exposing the actions of Comcast and pressuring the company to remove the restrictions. As such, BitTorrent has proven to be an invaluable ally to individual P2P users, despite the perception that Cohen has some-how sold out by remaking BitTorrent to attract corporate partners. Beyond indirectly fighting to allow P2P traffic to pass through networks unfet-tered by throttling or shaping, by forming these partnerships, BitTorrent has begun to legitimize P2P as a useful tool for purposes other than online piracy, demonstrating that the intellectual property industry can benefit from the advantages provided by P2P.

Even where partnerships between the groups have not been formed, there have been other recent attempts by both to create business models that touch on online piracy and digital content in some way. One model that appears to be poised to make the biggest impact is a social media center known as Boxee.[17] As media center software, Boxee allows users to play digital content through home televisions and stereo systems. Media center software has been available for years, in both open source and commercial varieties, but Boxee takes this a step further by allowing users to legally stream content available on television Web sites such as ComedyCentral.com. Additionally, Boxee adds a social component to typical media center functionality, allowing users to see what friends are watching and listening to and thus to determine what is popular in specific social circles. The connections to P2P lie in the roots of the Boxee project: the Xbox Media Center (XBMC). Boxee is an offshoot of the XBMC open source project, which provides free media center software that runs on the original Xbox video game console. Theoretically, a working (compiled) version of XBMC for the Xbox was illegal to distribute, given that it contained copyrighted software libraries and relied heavily on P2P for distribution. Additionally, while the software itself in no way facilitated piracy, it provided a means for pirated music and video to be played on televisions without restriction. As such, many users (like iPod users) have pirated significant amounts of the content for use with XBMC. In a way, Boxee is continuing along the trajectory first started by XBMC. While it is entirely legal to distribute Boxee, there are currently no good, legitimate sources of digital video content beyond what users rip themselves from their own legally purchased media. Given the choice between the tedious task of legitimately purchasing content then converting it to digital format, and quickly (but illegally) downloading content through P2P networks, it is unlikely that the majority of Boxee users will choose the less convenient option. So in a way, Boxee indirectly fuels online piracy in the absence of legitimate sources of (DRM-free) digital video, while at the same time attempting to make partnerships of its own with content providers.

Tools that have either actively facilitated online piracy or provide the platforms that allow pirated content to be played are slowly gaining legitimacy in the business world. As these types of tools legitimize P2P and digital content technologies, they actively begin to defend the spaces in which they operate from those attempting to stifle P2P use. While this may appear to make these new tools, and the businesses that created them, the allies of P2P users everywhere, it is unlikely that they would officially condone any use of their products for purposes that might in some way violate copyright. In the past, many have claimed that P2P represents the dominant business model of the future, but I'm not entirely convinced that I agree—despite organizations such as BitTorrent and Boxee. These types of businesses may preserve the infrastructure that allows for P2P, but they additionally provide a means by which the traditional intellectual property industry might remake P2P technologies into something new. In many ways, what is happening today with some of the P2P and digital content developers is similar to what happened in the 1970s with the Homebrew Computer Club: the commitments to free and open access to information are being slowly forgotten, as hobbyist projects become big business (see Chapter 3).

CONCLUSION

Millions of people are currently online, using P2P networks to share billions of files containing copyrighted music, movies, and software, and I expect that this number will only grow as the number of Internet users in the world increases. A consistently increasing user base, however, does not make for the unstoppable juggernaut which some more vocal Internet users make P2P and online piracy out to be. Unbeknownst to the majority of P2P users, there is something of a silent battle going on behind the scenes between P2P developers and users, on one side, and the intellectual property industry and device manufacturers, on the other. Currently it may appear that the P2P users are winning, but those who control the technologies that define the environment in which online piracy takes place are likely to have the final say on the matter, regardless of the flaws in copyright law. While online piracy will never entirely cease to exist, it is not entirely far-fetched to think that the intellectual property industry and device manufacturers will make it just inconvenient enough to prevent average Internet users from choosing to pirate digital content. Once that happens, online piracy in the United States will largely become a nonissue.

While I may have placed the actions of the intellectual property industry in something of a negative light, I unquestionably support the important protections provided by copyright in U.S. law. That said, there is a place for certain forms of piracy in the everyday life of media producers and consumers, as there always has been historically.[18] A crackdown on online piracy taken too far leads us into a situation where creativity and innovation are stifled. Despite the fact that Congress may lack the technical expertise to regulate Internet technologies that facilitate piracy in a usefully nuanced way, they undoubtedly realize that given the history of piracy in our country, there are legitimate reasons to maintain at least some acceptable level of online copyright violation. To an extent, in our current legislative, technical, and social environment, we already have exactly that. There exists a delicate tension between powerful copyright holders protecting their rights and the millions of P2P users benefiting from the violation of copyright. Currently, Congress and the courts are effectively faced with a decision to regulate P2P use out of existence or to exclude P2P use from copyright protections. Making either one of these decisions would create a huge imbalance of power between copyright holder and consumer. So, for nearly a decade, Congress has done neither. This has created a situation in which sharing copyrighted works is a violation of law, but enforcing that law is extremely difficult. In this way, infringing P2P use has become a popular, but ultimately risky, behavior—like speeding on the highway. The majority of speeders go unpunished, but without a law that limits speeding, everyone would do it. At this point, nearly everyone knows that using P2P to share copyrighted content is illegal, and that public knowledge has placed additional pressure on P2P users to pay for the content they receive. Obviously, not all actually do, but that pressure helps to keep the number of lost sales manageable. I readily admit that the situation is far from perfect, with the intellectual property industry (potentially) losing billions of dollars per year and individual file sharers in constant danger of hundred-thousand-dollar lawsuits, but at the very least, it is functional, if not always consistently fair, for both sides.[19]

Hopefully, through the course of this book, I've answered most of your questions about online piracy; at the very least, I've provided all the information that every computer user needs to know, along with a brief glimpse into the larger context in which online piracy occurs. In closing, if you do choose to use P2P networks in violation of copyright law, be careful out there, and keep a low profile. A brush with the intellectual property industry will never be a pleasant experience. Try to keep in mind that the struggle between consumers and copyright holders is far less black and white than either side may make it out to be. Be critical about the claims people and organizations make about online piracy and digital copyright issues. Regardless of what the future might bring for online piracy, develop and know your own stance on what is or is not acceptable use of P2P networks in your own home; whatever might be happening out in the world, your local actions and perceptions are what matter most in the end.

Appendix A

FULL INTERVIEW TRANSCRIPTS

JOHN: STUDENT TARGETED BY THE RECORDING
INDUSTRY ASSOCIATION OF AMERICA
(SPOKEN INTERVIEW)

NF: *So, who are you? What's your age, your background, etc . . . ?*

J: I am 20 years old, soon to be 21, I'm a junior at [a northeast college] study-ing biomedical engineering.

NF: *How and when did you get involved in P2P use?*

J: I actually, I think I was ahead of the curve, because, rather than AIM—you know America Online, they had the chat rooms—they had those servers where they would send you their list [of files being shared]. I don't know exactly what it was called, but . . .

NF: *I know exactly what you're talking about . . .*

J: I started back then, I was probably early teens, I would say. So, mid to late nineties.

NF: *Did anyone teach you how to do that, or did you just figure it out?*

J: I didn't even know these chat rooms existed, but once I discovered them, I kind of taught myself how to be come efficient at it. So, in a sense, I did teach myself, but I would have never known this whole subculture existed unless one of my friends showed me.

NF: *So what clients or networks are you currently using?*

J: Nothing now! <laughter> I think Limewire, KaZaA, Napster . . . that was a little further back, that would probably be what came after the online chat rooms. And then there was that whole dispute with Napster being sued, I moved on to KaZaA and Limewire, BearShare. And then, I used those for a little while until I came to ***, where I was introduced to torrents. So, I think I discovered that my sophomore year. So I started using things like BitComet, BitTorrent, and Azureus.

NF: *In the events leading up to the lawsuit, was BitTorrent your primary network?*

J: Yeah, BitComet, yeah.

NF: *Did you use any kind of firewall or IP blacklisting software?*

J: I don't even know what those are! <laughter>

NF: *So did you figure out BitTorrent on your own, or did somebody teach you?*

J: It was probably a similar situation, where someone mentioned it to me and I learned how to be efficient at it and use it on my own, using guides on the Web.

NF: *What types of media did you download and share, specifically leading up to the lawsuit.*

J: Well, I only ever downloaded songs and videos. I wouldn't like to download the movies in the theaters at the time, because they were always poor quality, so I downloaded ones that had come out on DVD. I would always do those and music files.

NF: *Did you try to keep up any sharing ratio on BitTorrent at all?*

J: I wasn't really concerned with it, but I also didn't block my stuff from being shared.

NF: *So how much would you say per year you downloaded?*

J: I probably downloaded a couple albums a week, so about 104 albums a year. And about 3 movies a week, so . . .

NF: *How often would you say you had a file-sharing client running on your computer?*

J: It definitely fluctuated, but I think one of the reasons I got caught was I would try to download on the *** network, so when I was studying or in class, I would be downloading something in the background. But, when I was off campus, I wouldn't really download anything.

NF: *How frequently did you see other people downloading and sharing? Was it common?*

J: Oh, it's *very* common. I can't believe how common it is, it seems like everyone does it.

NF: *How did you feel, prior to being sued, about the ethics of file sharing? Did you rationalize doing it in any way?*

J: I knew it was illegal, but in my eyes it didn't seem like that much of a crime. Maybe because it seemed like everyone was doing it. I guess I rationalized it by thinking that the record company and artists are already making millions. And, they were so readily available, it just seemed so convenient to do.

NF: *After being sued, did that change your opinion at all?*

J: I would have to say no, but I also am a reasonable person and I'm not going to take the risk, because I think I might be on a watch list or something . . .

NF: *That's unlikely, but we can talk about that later. . . . Did you ever feel pressure to get involved with file sharing?*

J: I didn't feel pressured, but [everyone doing it] made it feel like it was less wrong.

NF: *Who specifically brought a case against you?*

J: At first I wasn't even aware of who specifically it was, with all the legal terms I was a little bit confused. But, every company that the RIAA represents. It was only about music, which was surprising to me because I thought if someone was to bring a case against me that movies would be more expensive.

NF: *Well, they're actually two different organizations. . . . Did you know anything about the RIAA prior to the case, and what do you think of them now?*

J: Before, I didn't know the RIAA was their name, or who they represented, or what they did, but I knew there was some collaboration of bigwigs. When I found out about them I did my Googling and my research. I was actually abroad in Australia when I received an e-mail from the dean of students warning me that the RIAA had subpoenaed my information. So, right then, before I even knew it, I was actually going to be sued. Now, I'm not particularly fond of them, but I see where they're coming from.

NF: *What content were you sharing specifically that lead them to you?*

J: Well, they said it was 502 audio files, but they only listed 8 particular songs.

NF: *Did they catch you on BitTorrent specifically?*

J: I looked at the time of year, or the date they recorded the list of eight songs, and about that time I was using BitTorrent.

NF: *How did you know you were being sued?*

J: My father called and told me he had received a packet of documents and a letter from the RIAA saying they were going to sue me unless I wanted to settle.

NF: *How did the university react to the case that was brought against you?*

J: Well, at ***, me and 18 other students were swept up by one subpoena. I suppose that's what they can do, and that's why they target universities. I mean, I didn't really talk to too many *** officials. Other than, I visited the *** Union lawyer for some free consultation.

NF: *How did your friends react?*

J: I talked to my friends at ***, and they were like "Aw man, that sucks!" Pretty much everywhere they said, "I can't believe that happened, I can't believe it happened to you!" and "That really exists?!?" Then when I told them I had to fork over $4,000, they felt pretty bad for me.

NF: *Did they stop because of what happened to you?*

J: No, they kept doing it anyway.

NF: *How did your family react?*

J: Um, they felt it was unfortunate that I got caught, but I don't think they were disappointed in me because they also benefited from it. I would make them CDs for Christmas and birthdays. My dad loved all the oldies I would make for him. They were very supportive, they helped me do research on the RIAA and stuff.

NF: *They gave you a settlement offer, and you said you paid $4,000, correct?*

J: Well, apparently if I had settled immediately, it would have been a lot less, but I was in Australia so I couldn't actually settle. I also tried to kind of avoid it and postpone it, but after doing my research I found out that's why it increased. The final settlement was $4,100, and I know if I had settled a week earlier it would have been $4,000. But if I had settled way back when they first contacted me, I think it would have been $3,000.

NF: *Did you feel like you had any other option other than settling the case?*

J: Um, no. It seemed like they didn't want to give me any information. I got a number for the lawyer representing the RIAA, and I called, but whenever I would ask a question they would only say, "I'm not at liberty to say, I'm only a representative." They just weren't very helpful at all. I didn't expect them to provide me with a way to minimize how much I would pay them, but I was just curious about what was going on officially. I didn't see any of them face-to-face, and my Dad actually wondered if it was a scam at first. All the paperwork was sent to me via e-mail.

NF: *Is this process over for you now, or is there something more you have to do?*

J: Well, I paid my check last month, but they said I had to stop downloading and that I had to get rid of all the music I downloaded.

NF: *Do you plan on downloading in the future?*

J: Definitely not with programs, but I've found a Web site where you can get free mix tapes. The site doesn't really seem to know whether it's legal to do or not, but it seems legitimate.

NF: *Anything else that you want to add?*

J: On a personal note, it seems like they realized they couldn't stop illegal downloading, so they just wanted to capitalize on people's downloading. And rather than pay all those fees in court, they want you to pay the settlement so they can make a quick buck.

WAREZ SCENE MEMBER (E-MAIL INTERVIEW)

NF: *To begin with, give us your "pirate resume" so to speak. What scenes and what groups were you involved with, and when?*

M: I started BBS Warez around 1993, trading games and BBS software and applications for DOS. After that I found out about the Internet and obtained a Netcom account (notable because they were one of the companies Kevin Mitnick hacked), and started using Usenet to get software. If I remember correctly this was in 1995. From Usenet I progressed to IRC and Web sites, I actually ran a small HPAVC [hacking, phreaking, anarchy, virus, cracking] site for a time. Eventually, I was hanging out in warez IRC channels on efnet and various private networks, trading files. I actually ended up writing my own software to automate the sharing of my collection.

That situation continued right up until I entered college in 1999, at which point I gained access to true high-bandwidth connections. I made some friends on campus with interests and was introduced to some members of the anime fansub group AVCD (anime video CD) on IRC. We quickly put together a server using spare parts and put it on the campus network. We ran a top-tier anime fansub distribution site, which gave us access to all sorts of other content. At this point it's probably best to provide a quick overview of how any release group is organized.

At the top you have the heads and founders of the group, a position which is comparable to a corporation's CEO and board. They make decisions about policy and work to organize the efforts of the various internal departments.

After the main leadership, we come to the various working parts:

- Subbers—anime needs to be subtitled for English consumption

- Crackers—a lot of software has copy protection or registration keys, these people bypass all of that for the group

- Suppliers—at some point, be it software or anime, someone has to get a copy of it. These people generally trade what they can provide in order

- Site admins—responsible for maintaining and configuring the distribution servers

- Site hosts—someone with a high-bandwidth connection willing to have a fairly loud power hog of a server running

- Couriers—responsible for uploading the releases to various distribution sites (the truckers of the pirate world)

After about two years of running the AVCD distro server, I met someone from Razor1911. He set me up as the main U.S. distro for that group. They provided new server equipment in return for hosting and maintaining the server. Through them I gained access to sites in Europe and China containing a treasure trove of stuff.

I ran that server for Razor1911 until mid-2003, having survived a few different U.S. dragnets for pirate groups. I consider myself lucky and paranoid.

NF: *How was it that you became involved with the warez scene?*

 M: Boredom and curiosity. I had moved into a new region and was bored, so I started playing with the family computer. From that point on I learned of networks, modems, and bulletin boards. Each month yielded interactions with interesting new people.

NF: *How was it that you came to move about the scene—between groups and across roles? Who "promoted" you to higher positions, who accepted you into groups, and why?*

 M: Generally you met people on IRC and discussed roles. You would be introduced to the founders or administrators of a group. They would then vet you and give you access.

NF: *What were the benefits of being part of the scene?*

 M: Knowledge, experience, and connections. I would describe my experiences with the scene as providing me with my first corporate foray. I learned a lot about computer systems administration. In addition to the practical experiences, I gained access to a fairly expensive software, allowing me to learn how to use it and apply it. Access is a major benefit in my mind as most people don't create and set up their own Windows networks until they go to school. They also don't get experience with the different management and analytical tools until their professional career begins. Even in their professional careers it is unlikely that they will have as much access to the different tools as I did. I cannot emphasize enough how much of an advantage this is in the modern workplace where the work is increasingly knowledge oriented.

NF: *What were the negative aspects of being part of the scene?*

M: The possibility of arrest.

NF: *Tell me a little bit about what an average day in the scene was like for you.*

M: Basically I would wake up and hang out in an IRC channel when I was free. The couriers had more day-to-day work. Suppliers and crackers also did a good bit of work.

For a short while I worked as a supplier, someone would pay for a game to be delivered to me on its release day. It would be express shipped to me, and I would have contacted the parcel service in order to get the shipment as quickly as possible. In the scene speed was, and still is key, the first group to release a working copy of the goods won. It was my job to upload a copy of the game as fast as possible to our group distribution site. After that had been done, it was up to our cracking team to create whatever cracks were required. After the cracks were created it was my job to package the release and upload it to our primary distribution servers.

NF: *What were the relationships like within the groups there? What kinds of people did you meet, how close were you to them? Did you have any enemies?*

M: I would describe them as small office relationships, there might be one or two people that I would have stronger ties to.

I qualified the relationships as "small office," because communication was clear and very open. Everyone was on the same team, the only animosity and competition came from interactions with other groups.

Most of the people I interacted with were smart and technically savvy to some degree.

NF: *Were you ever "caught" by any authority figures? Parents? Intellectual property industry? ISPs? What happened?*

M: I've had my connections shut off due to "excessive" usage. Many companies like to advertise and sell "unlimited" data plans, but the reality of the situation is they oversell their capacity and then have to crack down on people actually attempting to use the bandwidth for anything other than basic Web browsing (that does not include things like YouTube).

NF: *Did you ever really leave the scene? If so, why? Does having been a part of all of that still benefit or hurt you in some way today? How?*

M: I consider myself retired. I no longer have access to top-level 0-day sites. I [still download] anime and TV shows from newsgroups and torrents. I will note that the producers of content are trying new tactics that make piracy less appealing. Consider Hulu [a free Internet streaming television service], I don't mind watching commercials in programs, as long as I can watch the program on my schedule.

I can certainly say that the experiences gained from my time in the scene benefit. My knowledge of technology would not be as expansive had I not been involved.

NF: *Knowing what you know about the scene today, what percentage (estimate) of pirated content originates from the scene?*

M: That really depends on the content. Software, I would say 90 percent. I'm sure there are some people out there sharing things via BitTorrent that aren't involved in the scene. The involvement with software is high due to the specialized nature of software cracking.

With regard to movies, television shows, and music, the barrier to participation is much lower. You only need to have access to the original content in some fashion to be able to contribute.

Fansubs are another category entirely as they generally aren't even available for viewing in the United States until months or years after their original showing on television.

Appendix B

RESOURCES AND INFORMATION

These Web sites were accessed between August and November 2008, and in the time following the publication of this book, they may have changed or been taken down. In such cases, I suggest entering the URL into the Internet archive (http://www.archive.org) or try using a search engine.

HISTORY

Textfiles.com

A Web site that has archived the messages and files once hosted on underground electronic bulletin board systems, including many pirate sites
http://www.textfiles.com/

"The Hacker Crackdown," by Bruce Sterling

A history of the computer underground during the 1980s and early 1990s, as written by one of the greatest cyberpunk authors
http://www.gutenberg.org/etext/101

***BBS: The Documentary,* by Jason Sadofsky**

A documentary on bulletin board system (BBS) culture and history, filmed and produced by BBS historian Jason Sadofsky, who also operates Textfiles.com
http://www.bbsdocumentary.com/

TECHNOLOGY

Azureus/Vuse
The most popular BitTorrent client
http://azureus.sourceforge.net/

Boxee
Social media center software that allows for the playback of legitimate and pirated content on home entertainment systems
http://blog.boxee.tv/

"How BitTorrent Works (Explained with Cardboard Cutouts)"
A brief video on how BitTorrent works
http://blog.managednetworks.co.uk/it-support/how-bittorrent-works-explained-with-cardboard-people/

"How Internet Infrastructure Works"
A brief guide to TCP/IP and the Internet
http://computer.howstuffworks.com/internet-infrastructure.htm

ONLINE SAFETY

"How Not to Get Sued for File Sharing," by the Electronic Frontier Foundation (EFF)
A guide on reducing the probability of being sued for online piracy
http://www.eff.org/pages/how-not-get-sued-file-sharing

PeerGuardian 2
IP address blacklisting software, which theoretically blocks the addresses of the intellectual property industry and government
http://phoenixlabs.org/pg2/

RESEARCH AND STATISTICS

Business Software Association's (BSA) 2007 Global Piracy Study
Results of the Business Software Association's annual piracy study
http://w3.bsa.org/globalstudy/

Cyber Safety and Ethics Initiative

The initiative started by Dr. Samuel McQuade to research youth computer abuse and provide the community with training and information on cyber safety

http://www.rrcsei.org/

Pew Internet and American Life Project

One of the largest private groups studying Internet use in America, with free data, reports, and statistics

http://www.pewinternet.org/

"The Effect of File Sharing on Record Sales: An Empirical Analysis," by Felix Oberholzer-Gee and Koleman Strumpf

A study on P2P file sharing, which indicates little damage to the recording industry

http://www.unc.edu/~cigar/papers/FileSharing_June2005_final.pdf

LAW

"Recording Industry vs. the People," by Ray Beckerman

The most comprehensive site for information on the Recording Industry Association of America court cases, including an index of lawyers willing to defend P2P users, court documents, and current news

http://recordingindustryvspeople.blogspot.com/

"Codev2 by Lawrence Lessig"

A discussion on the ways in which cyberspace is regulated—including online piracy—by one of the top U.S. cyberlaw scholars

http://codev2.cc/

"File Sharing," by EFF

A site documenting the efforts of the EFF to make file sharing legal and safe, while remaining profitable for artists

http://www.eff.org/issues/file-sharing

Free Culture, by Lawrence Lessig

Lessig's work on the relationships between online piracy, the regulation of cyberspace, and the intellectual property industry

http://www.amazon.com/Free-Culture-Technology-Control-Creativity/
dp/1594200068

Pirates of the Digital Millennium, by John Gantz and Jack Rochester

A more detailed analysis of the battle between various stakeholders over online piracy

http://www.amazon.com/Pirates-Digital-Millennium-Intellectual-Property/dp/0131463152

U.S. Copyright Office

Complete with guides and reference material concerning copyright law
http://copyright.gov/

INTELLECTUAL PROPERTY INDUSTRY

BSA

Trade association for software developers
http://www.bsa.org/

Motion Picture Association of America

Trade association for the movie industry
http://www.mpaa.org/

Recording Industry Association of America

Trade association for the recording industry
http://www.riaa.org/

Appendix C

ONLINE PIRACY TIMELINE

1600s	John Fell, Bishop of Oxford, coins the term *piracy*
1963	Bell Labs develops the first telephone modem
1967	Lawrence G. Roberts publishes ARPANET plans
1969	First ARPANET connections made between Stanford University and the University of California, Los Angeles
1975	ARPANET grows to 75 nodes
March	Homebrew Computer Club forms
June	Paper tape copy of MITS Altair BASIC stolen from Micro-Soft (now Microsoft) demonstration
July	First documented digital piracy incident: paper tape copies of MITS Altair BASIC are distributed at the Homebrew Computer Club
1976	Copyright Act passed, providing the current basis for U.S. copyright law
February	Bill Gates (Micro-Soft) writes an open letter to computer hobbyists demanding that the copies of MITS Altair BASIC no longer be distributed
1977	DC Hayes publicly releases the first cross-platform-compatible modem
1979, February	Ward Christensen and Randy Suess put first the bulletin board system (CBBS) online in Chicago, Illinois

1982   *Time* magazine names the PC "Person of the Year"

1983   *WarGames* is released in theaters

December   Wave of new PC users floods the BBS network

1985   Approximately 4,000 BBS are online in the United States

                         File Transfer Protocol (FTP) is formalized as an Internet protocol

1988   Jarkko Oikarinen develops Internet Relay Chat (IRC)

1989   Acceptable use policy restrictions lifted on the Internet, allowing public use

1991   Tim Berners-Lee announces the World Wide Web project

1993   Marc Andreessen releases the Mosaic Web browser

                         Moving Pictures Expert Group develops the MP3 audio standard

                         David LaMacchia opens the Cynosure pirate BBS at the Massachusetts Institute of Technology and is charged with wire fraud in the absence of appropriate copyright law

1994   CompuServe, America Online, GEnie, and Prodigy allow subscribers access to the Internet

1995   *The Net* and *Hackers* are released in theaters

                         Fraunhofer Society releases the first MP3 compression software and coins the term *MP3*

1996   Microsoft and Novell obtain a $70,000 settlement from the Assassin's Guild BBS sysop

                         First civil file-sharing lawsuit, *Software Publishers Association (SPA) vs. Max Butler,* is brought to court for sharing copyrighted files via FTP

                         Recording Industry Association of America (RIAA) begins to recognize file sharing as a threat and begins contacting "Internet music archive site" administrators, located primarily on college campuses

                         Shawn Fanning begins learning to program computers

1997   No Electronic Theft Act passed

                         Federal Bureau of Investigation organizes Operation Cyberstrike, targeting pirate BBS

June   RIAA begins suing administrators of "Internet music archive sites"

1998	Digital Millennium Copyright Act passed
1999, September	Shawn Fanning releases a beta version of Napster, which is quickly spread to 3,000 users
December	RIAA first attempts to sue Napster
2000, March	First Gnutella client is developed and released by Tom Pepper and Justin Frankel
July	Congressional hearing "Music on the Internet: Is There an Upside to Downloading?" is held
September	Jed McCaleb announces the eDonkey2000 P2P network
October	Napster boasts 32 million users, growing at a rate of 1 million users per month
October	*A&M Records, Inc. v. Napster, Inc.* case begins
2001, February	*A&M Records, Inc. v. Napster, Inc.* case is decided in favor of A&M Records
March	Niklas Zennström, Janus Friis, and Jaan Tallinn announce the FastTrack P2P network
May	Congressional hearing "Music and the Internet" is held
July	Bram Cohen announces the BitTorrent P2P network
July	Napster shuts down
September	Limewire, an open source Gnutella client, is released
2002	Andrej Preston creates Suprnova.org, considered one of the largest BitTorrent sites
September	Congressional hearing "Piracy of Intellectual Property on Peer-to-Peer Networks" is held
2003, February	Congressional hearing "Peer-to-Peer Piracy on University Campuses" is held
September	RIAA announces the first round of 261 civil law suits against P2P users
September	Twelve-year-old Brianna LaHara becomes the first P2P user to settle with the RIAA
November	Peter Sunde, Gottfrid Svartholm, and Fredrik Neij start ThePirateBay.org BitTorrent site in Sweden
2004	Suprnova.org is closed because of legal threats
October	Congressional hearing "Peer-to-Peer Piracy on University Campuses: An Update" is held

2005, March	*MGM Studios, Inc. v. Grokster, Ltd* case begins
June	*MGM Studios, Inc. v. Grokster, Ltd* case is decided in favor of MGM Studios
September	Congressional hearing "Reducing Peer-to-Peer (P2P) Piracy on University Campuses" is held
2006, May	Swedish police raid the ThePirateBay.org servers
2008	Number of RIAA legal threats against P2P users is estimated to total over 30,000
October	PRO-IP Act passed, increasing criminal penalties for copyright violation

NOTES

CHAPTER 1

1. Adrian Johns, *The Nature of the Book: Print and Knowledge in the Making* (Chicago: University of Chicago Press, 1998).

2. For an excellent discussion and critique of the concept of intellectual property, see Lawrence Lessig, *Free Culture: How Big Media Uses Technology and the Law to Lock Down Culture and Control Creativity* (New York: Penguin Press, 2004), chap. 1.

3. *USA Today*, "Peer-to-Peer Networks Unveil Code of Conduct," September 29, 2003, http://www.usatoday.com/tech/news/techpolicy/2003-09-29-p2p-code_x.htm.

4. Edna Gundersen, "Piracy Has Its Hooks In," *USA Today*, May 6, 2003, http://www.usatoday.com/life/music/news/2003-05-05-piracy-cover_x.htm.

5. Jefferson Graham, "RIAA Lawsuits Bring Consternation, Chaos," *USA Today*, September 10, 2003, http://www.usatoday.com/tech/news/techpolicy/2003-09-10-riaa-suit-reax_x.htm.

6. John Gantz and Jack B. Rochester, *Pirates of the Digital Millennium: How the Intellectual Property Wars Damage Our Personal Freedoms, Our Jobs, and the World Economy* (Upper Saddle River, NJ: Prentice Hall/Financial Times, 2005).

CHAPTER 2

1. Jason Scott, director, *BBS: The Documentary*, DVD (Cambridge, MA: Bovine Ignition Systems, 2005).

2. Laurence Pulgram, "Brief Amici Curiae of Innovation Scholars and Economists in Support of Affirmance, *EFF MGM v. Grokster,*" http://w2.eff.org/IP/P2P/MGM_v_Grokster/20050301_innovation.pdf.

3. Michele Boldrin and David Levine, "Against Intellectual Monopoly," http://levine.sscnet.ucla.edu/general/intellectual/against.htm.

4. Clinton Heylin, *Bootleg: The Secret History of the Other Recording Industry* (New York: St. Martin's Griffin, 1996).

5. Steven Levy, *Hackers: Heroes of the Computer Revolution,* 10th ed. (London: Penguin Books, 2001).

6. Ibid.

7. MITS, *MITS Altair BASIC Reference Manual* (Albuquerque, NM: MITS, 1975), http://www.swtpc.com/mholley/Altair/Introduction.pdf.

8. Levy, *Hackers.*

9. I may be criticized here for overemphasizing the role of the Homebrew Computer Club in the development of the personal computer. Yes, the big engineering firms, such as IBM and DEC, also played their own significant roles, but for the purposes of online piracy, the Homebrew Computer Club and the reconstitution of the hacker ethic are significantly more important.

10. Scott, *BBS: The Documentary.*

11. Harold Schneider, producer, *WarGames,* DVD, directed by John Badham (Santa Monica, CA: United Artists, 2008).

12. Bruce Sterling, *The Hacker Crackdown: Law and Disorder on the Electronic Frontier* (New York: Bantam Books, 1992).

13. Scott, *BBS: The Documentary.*

14. Ibid.

15. Sterling, *Hacker Crackdown.*

16. Ibid.

17. These are most certainly overgenereralized uses of the terms *hacker* and *phreak,* the true meanings of which are highly contested. As much as I enjoy discussing the use and travels of those terms, I have chosen here to avoid that particular controversy and instead embrace the popularized meanings that they have been assigned.

18. Sterling, *Hacker Crackdown.*

19. Scott, *BBS: The Documentary.*

20. Tim Berners-Lee, "WorldWideWeb: Summary," Alt.hypertext, message posted August 6, 1991, http://groups.google.com/group/alt.hypertext/msg/395f282a67a1916c?pli=1.

21. Ipggi, "A History of the Scene," http://www.rajuabju.com/warezirc/scene_history.htm.

22. Microsoft, "Novell and Microsoft Settle Largest BBS Piracy Case Ever," http://www.microsoft.com/presspass/press/1996/jan96/msnovpr.mspx.

23. Peter Beruk, "SPA Moves against Internet Pirate," Software and Information Industry Association, http://web.archive.org/web/19970109090233/www.spa.org/piracy/releases/butler3.htm.

24. K. V. Di Gregory, "Statement of Kevin V. Di Gregory Deputy Assistant Attorney General Criminal Division United States Department of Justice before

the Subcommittee on Courts and Intellectual Property Committee on the Judiciary United States House of Representatives Concerning H.R. 2265—The 'No Electronic Theft (Net) Act' Presented on September 11, 1997," U.S. Department of Justice, http://www.usdoj.gov/criminal/cybercrime/tesfin.htm.

25. Ipggi, "A History of the Scene."

26. Fraunhofer IIS, "The MP3 History 03," http://www.iis.fraunhofer.de/EN/bf/amm/mp3history/mp3history03.jsp.

27. Jonathan Lamy, "Recording Industry Protects Copyrighted Sound Recordings on the Internet," Recording Industry Association of America, http://www.riaa.com/newsitem.php?news_month_filter=6&news_year_filter=1997&resultpage=&id=8B093A65-D114–01FD-D929-EA666124F8EE.

28. Trevor Merriden, *Irresistible Forces: The Business Legacy of Napster and the Growth of the Underground Internet* (Oxford: Capstone, 2001).

29. Julian Dibbell, "Immaterial World," Idée Fixe, http://web.archive.org/web/20010303124901/http://www.feedmag.com/feature/cx329lofi.html.

CHAPTER 3

1. Not all computers use what is known as Dynamic Host Configuration Protocol (DHCP) to receive an address when they connect to a network. Computers may also have what is known as a static IP address, meaning that it never changes. However, the majority of ISPs use DHCP to assign an address from a pool of addresses to computers when they connect.

2. One of the best examples of this is the rise of DVD ripper/encoder "aXXo," whose releases can be found on nearly every BitTorrent tracker and P2P network.

3. Compression and encoding are effectively the same thing: both processes use mathematical algorithms to reduce the size of any given file. When someone wishes to then play the encoded or compressed content, the computer must decode the algorithm to play the content back, requiring a certain amount of computing resources. The difference between encoding and compression is that encoded files are compressed to the point to which an average computer may easily decode the content quickly enough to play the file without slowdown. This is not the case for compression, which takes a higher level of computing resources and is therefore too slow to allow the content to be played.

4. Martinez Kiyoshi, "Nothing's Gonna Stop the Flow," *Daily Illini,* July 2, 2005, http://media.www.dailyillini.com/media/storage/paper736/news/2005/02/07/features/nothings.gonna.stop.the.flow-854470-page2.shtml.

CHAPTER 4

1. Scott Gilbertson, "Feds Claim Internet Is One Percent Porn," Monkey Bites, posted November 16, 2006, http://blog.wired.com/monkeybites/2006/11/feds_claim_inte.html.

2. Graham Lee, "The NPD Group: Peer-to-Peer Digital Video Downloading Outpacing Legal Alternatives Five to One," NPD Group, http://www.npd.com/press/releases/press_061220.html.

3. U.S. General Accounting Office, "The Use of Peer-to-Peer Networks to Access Pornography," http://www.gao.gov/new.items/d05634.pdf.

4. Avi Baumstein, "Our P2P Investigation Turns Up Business Data Galore," *Information Week,* March 17, 2008, http://www.informationweek.com/news/security/cybercrime/showArticle.jhtml?articleID=206903417.

5. Gil Kaufman, "Madonna to Pirates: What the F— Do You Think You're Doing?" MTV News, http://www.mtv.com/news/articles/1471321/20030416/adonna.jhtml?headlines=true.

6. Robert Lemos, "Hired Gun Blamed for Business Outage," SecurityFocus, http://www.securityfocus.com/news/11521.

CHAPTER 5

1. Anon. "Download Music, Movies, Games, Software! The Pirate Bay— The World's Largest BitTorrent Tracker." November 5, 2008. http://thepirate bay.org/.

2. Mininova, "Statistics," http://www.mininova.org/statistics.

3. Thomas Mennecke, "P2P Population Remains Steady," Slyck News, http://www.slyck.com/story1314_P2P_Population_Remains_Steady.

4. Ernesto, "Filesharing Report Shows Explosive Growth for uTorrent," TorrentFreak, posted April 26, 2008, http://torrentfreak.com/p2p-statistics-080426/.

5. R. C. Hollinger, "Crime by Computer: Correlates of Software Piracy and Unauthorized Account Access," *Security Journal* 4, no. 1 (1993): 2–12.

6. W. F. Skinner and A. M. Fream, "A Social Learning Theory Analysis of Computer Crime among College Students," *Journal of Research in Crime and Delinquency* 34, no. 4 (1997): 495–518.

7. David Phelps, "SPA Anti-piracy Hot Spot Home Page," Software Publishers Association, http://web.archive.org/web/19970109082630/www.spa.org/piracy/releases/spa_bsa.htm.

8. Business Software Alliance, "Sixth Annual BSA Global Software Piracy Study," http://web.archive.org/web/20010917023709/www.bsa.org/resources/2001-05-21.55.pdf.

9. Business Software Alliance, "Second Annual BSA and IDC Global Software Piracy Study," http://w3.bsa.org/globalstudy//upload/2005-Global-Study-English.pdf.

10. Business Software Alliance, "Fifth Annual BSA and IDC Global Software Piracy Study," http://global.bsa.org/idcglobalstudy2007/studies/2007_global_piracy_study.pdf.

11. Business Software Alliance, "Survey Spotlights Growing Problem of On-line Software Piracy," http://web.archive.org/web/20030424034013/http://www.bsa.org/resources/2002-05-29.117.pdf.

12. Business Software Alliance, "Youth and Downloading," http://www.bsa.org/country/Research%20and%20Statistics/~/media/03EF7894F6A3488D97673F1B1BB29DCF.ashx.

13. Lee Rainie, "13 Million Americans 'Freeload' Music on the Internet; 1 Billion Free Music Files Now Sit on Napster Users' Computers," Pew Internet and American Life Project, http://www.pewinternet.org/pdfs/MusicReportFull.pdf.

14. Lee Rainie and Mary Madden, "Pew Internet Project and Comscore Media Metrix Data Memo," Pew Internet and American Life Project, http://www.pewin ternet.org/pdfs/PIP_File_Swapping_Memo_0104.pdf.

15. Ipsos, "Internet Piracy on Campus," http://www.bsa.org/country/Re search%20and%20Statistics/~/media/80B03498709F4B7E93E6B2D449795763. ashx.

16. Business Wire, "New Survey Indicates Parents Unaware of or Indifferent to Risks of Illegal File Swapping," March 17, 2004, http://findarticles.com/p/ articles/mi_m0EIN/is_/ai_114311029.

17. ttol, "Operation Buccaneer Updates," http://free.hostultra.com/~parazite/ scenebusts72.htm.

18. Samuel McQuade and Neel Sampat, "Report of the Rochester Institute of Technology Survey of Internet and At-risk Behaviors," Rochester Institute of Technology, http://www.rrcsei.org/RIT%20Cyber%20Survey%20Final%20Re port.pdf.

19. S. J. Liebowitz, "Will MP3 Downloads Annihilate the Record Industry? The Evidence So Far," http://papers.ssrn.com/sol3/papers.cfm?abstract_id=414162.

20. Ivan Png, "Copyright: A Plea for Empirical Research," *Review of Economic Research on Copyright Issues* 3, no. 2 (2006): 3–13.

21. F. Oberholzer-Gee and K. Strumpf, "The Effect of File Sharing on Record Sales: An Empirical Analysis," *Journal of Political Economy* 115, no. 1 (2007): 1–42.

22. F. Oberholzer-Gee, "Peer-to-Peer File-Sharing Technology: Consumer Protection and Competition Issues," paper presented at the FTC Peer-to-Peer File-Sharing Workshop, Washington, DC, December 15, 2004, http://www.ftc. gov/bcp/workshops/filesharing/.

23. David Blackburn, "The Heterogeneous Effects of Copying: The Case of Recorded Music," http://www.katallaxi.se/grejer/blackburn/blackburn_fs.pdf.

24. Motion Picture Association, "The Cost of Movie Piracy," http://www.mpaa. org/press_releases/leksummarympa.pdf.

25. Motion Picture Association, "The Cost of Movie Piracy," http://www.mpaa. org/press_releases/leksummarympa.pdf.

26. Box Office Mojo, "Yearly Box Office," http://www.boxofficemojo.com/ yearly/.

CHAPTER 6

1. James Burke, *The Day the Universe Changed* (Boston: Little, Brown, 1985).

2. Irving E. Fang, *A History of Mass Communication: Six Information Revolutions* (Boston: Focal Press, 1997).

3. Lewis Mumford, *Art and Technics* (New York: Columbia University Press, 1952).

4. H. R. Varian, "Copying and Copyright," *Journal of Economic Perspectives* 19, no. 2 (2005): 121–38.

5. P. E. Geller, "Copyright History and the Future: What's Culture Got to Do with It?" *Journal of the Copyright Society of the U.S.A.* 47 (1999): 209–64.

6. Interestingly, where the United States once balked at the Berne Convention, seeing the benefits that could arise from allowing Americans to ignore foreign copyright, the tables have now turned. The American intellectual property industry is currently one of the most successful in the world and accounts for 5 percent of the nation's gross domestic product. As such, while many nations voice assistance in protecting copyright on an international scale, their copyright policies are rarely enforced. In particular, Russia and China have rampant piracy problems, with music, movies, and software being pirated and sold at heavily reduced prices.

7. E. Goldman, "A Road to No Warez: The No Electronic Theft Act and Criminal Copyright Infringement," *Oregon Law Review* 82 (2003): 369–432.

8. Ibid.

9. Adrian Johns, *The Nature of the Book: Print and Knowledge in the Making* (Chicago: University of Chicago Press, 1998).

10. Arnold Lutzker, "Primer on the Digital Millennium," http://web.archive. org/web/20060710041612/http://www.arl.org/info/frn/copy/primer.html.

11. U.S. Copyright Office, "Copyright Office Basics," http://www.copyright. gov/circs/circ1.html.

12. Neil Wake, "*Atlantic Recording Corporation, et al., vs. Pamela and Jeffrey Howell,*" http://www.ilrweb.com/viewILRPDF.asp?filename=atlantic_ howell_ 080429Decision.

13. John Borland, "RIAA Sues 261 File Swappers," *CNET News*, September 8, 2003, http://news.cnet.com/2100-1023_3-5072564.html.

14. David Kravetz, "File Sharing Lawsuits at a Crossroads, after 5 Years of RIAA Litigation," Threat Level, posted September 4, 2008. http://blog.wired. com/27bstroke6/2008/09/proving-file-sh.html.

15. U.S. Department of Justice, "NET Act: 17 U.S.C. and 18 U.S.C. as Amended (Redlined)," http://www.usdoj.gov/criminal/cybercrime/17-18red.htm.

16. Jack Lerner, Laura Quilter, Jason Schultz, and Jennifer Urban, "Frequently Asked Questions (and Answers) about Anticrcumvention (DCMA)," Chilling Effects, http://www.chillingeffects.org/anticircumvention/faq.cgi#qid123.

17. U.S. Copyright Office, "Copyright and Digital Files," http://www.copy right.gov/help/faq/faq-digital.html.

18. Lawrence Lessig, *Free Culture: How Big Media Uses Technology and the Law to Lock Down Culture and Control Creativity* (New York: Penguin Press, 2004).

19. For the record, I'm not a fan of the DMCA—perhaps with the exception of safe harbor provisions.

CHAPTER 7

1. David Kravetz, "File Sharing Lawsuits at a Crossroads, after 5 Years of RIAA Litigation," Threat Level, posted September 4, 2008, http://blog.wired. com/27bstroke6/2008/09/proving-file-sh.html.

2. ttol, "Operation Buccaneer Updates," http://free.hostultra.com/~parazite/scenebusts72.htm.

3. U.S. Department of Justice, "Operation Buccaneer," Cybercrime.gov, http://www.cybercrime.gov/ob/OBMain.htm.

4. U.S. Department of Justice, "Twelve 'Operation Bandwidth' Software Pirates Enter into Group Guilty Plea (December 18, 2003)," http://www.usdoj.gov/criminal/cybercrime/bandwidthPlea.htm.

5. Ibid.

6. ttol, "Operation Buccaneer Updates."

7. John is not his real name.

8. Kai Ryssdal, "Marketplace: No Pause in Music Industry's Tough Play," American Public Media, http://marketplace.publicradio.org/display/web/2007/09/17/face_music_part1/.

9. Ray Beckerman, "Suggestions to College Students Being Targeted by the RIAA," Recording Industry vs. the People, http://recordingindustryvspeople.blogspot.com/2007/04/suggestions-to-college-students-being.html.

10. Trevor Merriden, *Irresistible Forces: The Business Legacy of Napster and the Growth of the Underground Internet* (Oxford: Capstone, 2001).

CHAPTER 8

1. E.g., Time Warner, which is an ISP, cable television provider, and movie studio.

2. Lawrence Lessig, *Free Culture: How Big Media Uses Technology and the Law to Lock Down Culture and Control Creativity* (New York: Penguin Press, 2004), p. 9.

3. Asher Moses, "Rivals Combine to Combat Crime," *Sydney Morning Herald,* October 29, 2008, http://www.smh.com.au/news/technology/biztech/kazaa-foes-join-up-to-fight-pirates-porn/2008/10/28/1224956013205.html.

4. Also referred to as digital restrictions management by critics.

5. Again, I'm glossing over quite a bit by calling all these groups of people hackers in an effort to simplify terminology.

6. Oopho2ei, "Finally Handling BD+ (?)," Doom9's Forum, message posted October 28, 2008, http://forum.doom9.org/showthread.php?p=1207578# post 1207578.

7. The Digital Douwd, "Closing Letter to the Copyright Industry Associations of America," The Big Hack, http://thebighack.org/modules.php?op=modload&name=News&file=article&sid=622&mode=nested&order=0&thold=0.

8. OFF System, The. "OFF System Introduction." http://offsystem.sourceforge.net/.

9. "Games Firms 'Catching' Non-gamers," *BBC News,* October 30, 2008, http://news.bbc.co.uk/1/hi/technology/7697898.stm.

10. Relakks, "Legal," https://www.relakks.com/faq/legal/.

11. As of November 2008.

12. Jaikumar Vijayan, "Oregon: Ground Zero in Fight between RIAA, Alleged Music Pirates?" *Computerworld Security,* November 30, 2007, http://www.computerworld.com/action/article.do?command=viewArticleBasic&articleId=9050319.

13. Corynne McSherry, "Capitol v. Thomas: Judge Orders New Trial, Implores Congress to Lower Statutory Penalties for P2P," Electronic Frontier Foundation, http://www.eff.org/deeplinks/2008/09/capitol-v-thomas-judge-orders-new-trial-implores-c.

14. Ray Beckerman, "Announcement from Harvard Law School Cyberlaw Students about SONY v. Tenenbaum," Recording Industry vs. the People, http://recordingindustryvspeople.blogspot.com/search?q=tenenbaum.

15. Richard Korman, "Harvard's Charlie Nesson Raises Constitutional Questions in RIAA Litigation," ZDNet Government. http://government.zdnet.com/?p=4152.

16. BitTorrent, "Partners," http://www.bittorrent.com/company/partners/.

17. Avner Ronen, "About," Boxee Blog, posted April 5, 2007, http://blog.boxee.tv/about/.

18. Lessig, *Free Culture.*

19. A functionalist argument, I know.

GLOSSARY

bandwidth capping. A limit set on the amount of network traffic that any given Internet user may send and receive in a given period of time.

BitTorrent. A P2P protocol that reduces bandwidth costs by distributing bandwidth across the number of computers requesting a given file.

bulletin board system (BBS). An electronic bulletin board system, popular during the 1980s and early 1990s, which allowed users to dial in via modem and communicate with other users, in addition to hosting files.

client. The software or computer that accesses a service hosted by another computer (server) via a network.

copyright. A set of rights given to authors guaranteeing them control over the copying, distribution, and performance of their work.

courier. Member of a warez group who distributes pirated content between top-level warez servers.

cracker. Member of a warez group who removes copyright protection from content in preparation for release to the warez scene and P2P networks.

digital piracy. The piracy of digital media content; does not imply the use of computer networks for distribution.

digital rights management (DRM). Technologies that prevent the unauthorized use of digital content, such as music, movies, and software. Occasionally referred to as Digital Restrictions Management.

encoder. Member of a warez group who converts raw audio or video data into compressed file formats such as MP3 or AVI files.

encoding. The act of converting raw audio or video data into compressed file formats such as MP3 or AVI files.

FTP. An abbreviation for File Transfer Protocol; a network protocol that allows users to transfer files between users using a client-server model.

Homebrew Computer Club. A group of computer enthusiasts formed in the 1970s, from which many early influential PC companies were formed; also the site of the first recorded incidence of digital piracy, when members copied and distributed paper tape versions of MITS Altair BASIC stolen from a Microsoft demonstration.

hybrid P2P networks. P2P networks that utilize centralized servers to manage users or index files.

intellectual property. The intangible result of creative work, including books, movies, images, and software, among other media.

intellectual property industry. Those organizations and individuals that produce and manage media content as a consumer good; includes the Recording Industry Association of America, the Motion Picture Association of America, and so on.

Internet Relay Chat (IRC). A protocol that allows for semianonymous chat rooms and file transfers.

internet service provider (ISP). A company that offers Internet connection service to homes and businesses; examples include Time Warner, Verizon, and NetZero.

Napster. A hybrid P2P system developed by Shaun Fanning in late 1999, primarily designed for sharing music among friends; it was the first system of its kind to become adopted quickly by millions of Internet users and was ordered to shut down in July 2001.

online piracy. The illegal copying and distribution of copyrighted digital works via the Internet.

peer-to-peer (P2P). A form of network architecture in which each computer in the network may act as a server for the others, either for the purposes of file sharing or for other forms of communication.

piracy. Slang for copyright infringement, which gained popularity prior to copyright laws; the act of copying and distributing intellectual property without authorization from the rights holder.

ripping. Copying the content of a CD or DVD onto a computer, usually implying some form of encoding into a compressed audio or video file format.

server. A computer on a network that provides services to other computers such as making files available for download.

shaping/packet shaping. A process of prioritizing specific types of network traffic over other types of network traffic; commonly used by Internet service providers to slow down P2P file transfers.

supplier. Member of a warez group who obtains a legitimate copy of the content to be released; methods of obtaining files include theft from producers, hacking into corporate networks, videotaping movies, and retail purchasing.

TCP/IP. The set of standards that govern the ways in which computers communicate with one another over a network such as the Internet.

traditional piracy. The illegal manufacturing and sales of copyrighted content; differentiated from online piracy in that physical copies of the content are sold to individuals at low cost.

true P2P networks. P2P networks that do not rely on a centralized server for either connection purposes or file indexing.

warez. Internet slang for pirated content.

BIBLIOGRAPHY

Baumstein, Avi. "Our P2P Investigation Turns Up Business Data Galore." *Information Week*, March 17, 2008, http://www.informationweek.com/news/security/cybercrime/showArticle.jhtml?articleID=206903417.

Beckerman, Ray. "Announcement from Harvard Law School Cyberlaw Students about SONY v. Tenenbaum." Recording Industry vs. the People. http://recordingindustryvspeople.blogspot.com/search?q=tenenbaum.

Beckerman, Ray. "Suggestions to College Students Being Targeted by the RIAA." Recording Industry vs. the People. http://recordingindustryvspeople.blogspot.com/2007/04/suggestions-to-college-students-being.html.

Berners-Lee, Tim. "WorldWideWeb: Summary." Alt.hypertext, message posted August 6, 1991. http://groups.google.com/group/alt.hypertext/msg/395f282a67a1916c?pli=1.

Beruk, Peter. "SPA Moves against Internet Pirate." Software and Information Industry Association. http://web.archive.org/web/19970109090233/www.spa.org/piracy/releases/butler3.htm.

BitTorrent. "Partners." http://www.bittorrent.com/company/partners/.

Blackburn, David. "The Heterogeneous Effects of Copying: The Case of Recorded Music." http://www.katallaxi.se/grejer/blackburn/blackburn_fs.pdf.

Boldrin, Michele, and David Levine. "Against Intellectual Monopoly." http://levine.sscnet.ucla.edu/general/intellectual/against.htm.

Borland, John. "RIAA Sues 261 File Swappers." *CNET News*, September 8, 2003, http://news.cnet.com/2100-1023_3-5072564.html.

Box Office Mojo. "Yearly Box Office." http://www.boxofficemojo.com/yearly/.

Burke, James. *The Day the Universe Changed.* Boston: Little, Brown, 1985.

Business Software Alliance. "Fifth Annual BSA and IDC Global Software Piracy Study." http://global.bsa.org/idcglobalstudy2007/studies/2007_global_piracy_study.pdf.

Business Software Alliance. "Second Annual BSA and IDC Global Software Piracy Study." http://w3.bsa.org/globalstudy//upload/2005-Global-Study-English.pdf.

Business Software Alliance. "Sixth Annual BSA Global Software Piracy Study." http://web.archive.org/web/20010917023709/www.bsa.org/resources/2001-05-21.55.pdf.

Business Software Alliance. "Survey Spotlights Growing Problem of Online Software Piracy." http://web.archive.org/web/20030424034013/http://www.bsa.org/resources/2002-05-29.117.pdf.

Business Software Alliance. "Youth and Downloading." http://www.bsa.org/country/Research%20and%20Statistics/~/media/03EF7894F6A3488D97673F1B1BB29DCF.ashx.

Business Wire. "New Survey Indicates Parents Unaware of or Indifferent to Risks of Illegal File Swapping." March 17, 2004, http://findarticles.com/p/articles/mi_m0EIN/is_/ai_114311029.

Dibbell, Julian. "Immaterial World." Idée Fixe. http://web.archive.org/web/20010303124901/http://www.feedmag.com/feature/cx329lofi.html.

Digital Douwd, The. "Closing Letter to the Copyright Industry Associations of America." Big Hack, The. http://thebighack.org/modules.php?op=modload&name=News&file=article&sid=622&mode=nested&order=0&thold=0.

Di Gregory, K. V. "Statement of Kevin V. Di Gregory Deputy Assistant Attorney General Criminal Division United States Department of Justice before the Subcommittee on Courts and Intellectual Property Committee on the Judiciary United States House of Representatives Concerning H.R. 2265—The 'No Electronic Theft (Net) Act' Presented on September 11, 1997." U.S. Department of Justice. http://www.usdoj.gov/criminal/cybercrime/tes fin.htm.

Ernesto. "Filesharing Report Shows Explosive Growth for uTorrent." TorrentFreak, posted April 26, 2008. http://torrentfreak.com/p2p-statistics-080426/.

Fang, Irving E. *A History of Mass Communication: Six Information Revolutions.* Boston: Focal Press, 1997.

Fraunhofer IIS. "The MP3 History 03." http://www.iis.fraunhofer.de/EN/bf/amm/mp3history/mp3history03.jsp.

"Games Firms 'Catching' Non-gamers." *BBC News,* October 30, 2008. http://news.bbc.co.uk/1/hi/technology/7697898.stm.

Gantz, John, and Jack B. Rochester. *Pirates of the Digital Millennium: How the Intellectual Property Wars Damage Our Personal Freedoms, Our Jobs, and the World Economy.* Upper Saddle River, NJ: Prentice Hall / Financial Times, 2005.

Geller, P. E. "Copyright History and the Future: What's Culture Got to Do with It?" *Journal of the Copyright Society of the U.S.A.* 47 (1999): 209–64.

Gilbertson, Scott. "Feds Claim Internet Is One Percent Porn." Monkey Bites, posted November 16, 2006, http://blog.wired.com/monkeybites/2006/11/feds_claim_inte.html.

Goldman, E. "A Road to No Warez: The No Electronic Theft Act and Criminal Copyright Infringement." *Oregon Law Review* 82 (2003): 369–432.

Graham, Jefferson. "RIAA Lawsuits Bring Consternation, Chaos." *USA Today,* September 10, 2003, http://www.usatoday.com/tech/news/techpolicy/2003-09-10-riaa-suit-reax_x.htm.

Gundersen, Edna. "Piracy Has Its Hooks In." *USA Today,* May 6, 2003, http://www.usatoday.com/life/music/news/2003-05-05-piracy-cover_x.htm.

Heylin, Clinton. *Bootleg: The Secret History of the Other Recording Industry.* New York: St. Martin's Griffin, 1996.

Hollinger, R. C. "Crime by Computer: Correlates of Software Piracy and Unauthorized Account Access." *Security Journal* 4, no. 1 (1993): 2–12.

Ipggi. "A History of the Scene." http://www.rajuabju.com/warezirc/scene_history.htm.

Ipsos. "Internet Piracy on Campus." http://www.bsa.org/country/Research%20and%20Statistics/~/media/80B03498709F4B7E93E6B2D449795763.ashx.

Johns, Adrian. *The Nature of the Book: Print and Knowledge in the Making.* Chicago: University of Chicago Press, 1998.

Kaufman, Gil. "Madonna to Pirates: What the F— Do You Think You're Doing?" MTV News. http://www.mtv.com/news/articles/1471321/20030416/madonna.jhtml?headlines=true.

Kiyoshi, Martinez. "Nothing's Gonna Stop the Flow." *Daily Illini,* July 2, 2005, http://media.www.dailyillini.com/media/storage/paper736/news/2005/02/07/features/nothings.gonna.stop.the.flow-854470-page2.shtml.

Korman, Richard. "Harvard's Charlie Nesson Raises Constitutional Questions in RIAA Litigation." ZDNet Government. http://government.zdnet.com/?p=4152.

Kravetz, David. "File Sharing Lawsuits at a Crossroads, after 5 Years of RIAA Litigation." Threat Level, posted September 4, 2008. http://blog.wired.com/27bstroke6/2008/09/proving-file-sh.html.

Lamy, Jonathan. "Recording Industry Protects Copyrighted Sound Recordings on the Internet." Recording Industry Association of America. http://www.riaa.com/newsitem.php?news_month_filter=6&news_year_filter=1997&resultpage=&id=8B093A65-D114–01FD-D929-EA666124F8EE.

Lee, Graham. "The NPD Group: Peer-to-Peer Digital Video Downloading Outpacing Legal Alternatives Five to One." NPD Group. http://www.npd.com/press/releases/press_061220.html.

Lemos, Robert. "Hired Gun Blamed for Business Outage." SecurityFocus. http://www.securityfocus.com/news/11521.

Lerner, Jack, Laura Quilter, Jason Schultz, and Jennifer Urban. "Frequently Asked Questions (and Answers) about Anticrcumvention (DCMA)." Chilling Effects. http://www.chillingeffects.org/anticircumvention/faq.cgi#qid123.

Lessig, Lawrence. *Free Culture: How Big Media Uses Technology and the Law to Lock Down Culture and Control Creativity.* New York: Penguin Press, 2004.

Levy, Steven. *Hackers: Heroes of the Computer Revolution.* 10th ed. London: Penguin Books, 2001.

Liebowitz, S. J. "Will MP3 Downloads Annihilate the Record Industry? The Evidence So Far." http://papers.ssrn.com/sol3/papers.cfm?abstract_id= 414162.

Lutzker, Arnold. "Primer on the Digital Millennium." http://web.archive.org/web/20060710041612/http://www.arl.org/info/frn/copy/primer.html.

McGuire, Michael. *Hypercrime: The New Geometry of Harm.* 1st ed. New York: Routledge-Cavendish, 2007.

McQuade, Samuel, and Neel Sampat. "Report of the Rochester Institute of Technology Survey of Internet and At-risk Behaviors." Rochester Institute of Technology. http://www.rrcsei.org/RIT%20Cyber%20Survey%20Final%20 Report.pdf.

McSherry, Corynne. "Capitol v. Thomas: Judge Orders New Trial, Implores Congress to Lower Statutory Penalties for P2P." Electronic Frontier Foundation. http://www.eff.org/deeplinks/2008/09/capitol-v-thomas-judge-orders-new-trial-implores-c.

Mennecke, Thomas. "P2P Population Remains Steady." Slyck News. http://www.slyck.com/story1314_P2P_Population_Remains_Steady.

Merriden, Trevor. *Irresistible Forces: The Business Legacy of Napster and the Growth of the Underground Internet.* Oxford: Capstone, 2001.

Microsoft. "Novell and Microsoft Settle Largest BBS Piracy Case Ever." http://www.microsoft.com/presspass/press/1996/jan96/msnovpr.mspx.

Mininova. "Statistics." http://www.mininova.org/statistics.

MITS. *MITS Altair BASIC Reference Manual.* Albequerque, NM: MITS, 1975, http://www.swtpc.com/mholley/Altair/Introduction.pdf.

Moses, Asher. "Rivals Combine to Combat Crime." *Sydney Morning Herald,* October 29, 2008, http://www.smh.com.au/news/technology/biztech/kazaa-foes-join-up-to-fight-pirates-porn/2008/10/28/1224956013205.html.

Motion Picture Association. "The Cost of Movie Piracy." http://www.mpaa.org/press_releases/leksummarympa.pdf.

Mumford, Lewis. *Art and Technics.* New York: Columbia University Press, 1952.

Oberholzer-Gee, F. "Peer-to-Peer File-Sharing Technology: Consumer Protection and Competition Issues." Paper presented at the FTC Peer-to-Peer File-Sharing Workshop, Washington, DC, December 15, 2004, http://www.ftc.gov/bcp/workshops/filesharing/.

Oberholzer-Gee, F., and K. Strumpf. "The Effect of File Sharing on Record Sales: An Empirical Analysis." *Journal of Political Economy* 115, no. 1 (2007): 1–42.

OFF System, The. "OFF System Introduction." http://offsystem.sourceforge.net/.

Oopho2ei. "Finally Handling BD+(?)." Doom9's Forum, message posted October 28, 2008. http://forum.doom9.org/showthread.php?p=1207578#post1207578.

Pember, Don R., and Clay Calvert. *Mass Media Law.* Boston: McGraw-Hill, 2004.

Phelps, David. "SPA Anti-piracy Hot Spot Home Page." Software Publishers Association. http://web.archive.org/web/19970109082630/www.spa.org/piracy/releases/spa_bsa.htm.

Png, Ivan. "Copyright: A Plea for Empirical Research." *Review of Economic Research on Copyright Issues* 3, no. 2 (2006): 3–13.

Pulgram, Laurence. "Brief Amici Curiae of Innovation Scholars and Economists in Support of Affirmance, *EFF MGM v. Grokster.*" http://w2.eff.org/IP/P2P/MGM_v_Grokster/20050301_innovation.pdf.

Rainie, Lee. "13 Million Americans 'Freeload' Music on the Internet; 1 Billion Free Music Files Now Sit on Napster Users' Computers." Pew Internet and American Life Project. http://www.pewinternet.org/pdfs/MusicReportFull.pdf.

Rainie, Lee, and Mary Madden. "Pew Internet Project and Comscore Media Metrix Data Memo." Pew Internet and American Life Project. http://www.pewinternet.org/pdfs/PIP_File_Swapping_Memo_0104.pdf.

Rampell, Catherine. "How It Does It: The RIAA Explains How It Catches Alleged Music Pirates." *Chronicle of Higher Education,* May 13, 2008, http://chronicle.com/free/2008/05/2821n.htm.

Recording Industry Association of America. "Recording Industry Protects Copyrighted Sound Recordings on the Internet." http://www.riaa.com/newsitem.php?news_year_filter=&resultpage=138&id=8B093A65-D114-01FD-D929-EA666124F8EE.

Relakks. "Legal." https://www.relakks.com/faq/legal/.

Reuters. "Inside the Music Industry's Piracy Battle." June 9, 2008, http://www.reuters.com/article/musicNews/idUSN0840383620080610.

Ronen, Avner. "About." Boxee Blog, posted April 5, 2007. http://blog.boxee.tv/about/.

Ryssdal, Kai. "Marketplace: No Pause in Music Industry's Tough Play." American Public Media. http://marketplace.publicradio.org/display/web/2007/09/17/face_music_part1/.

Schneider, Harold, producer. *WarGames.* DVD. Directed by John Badham. Santa Monica, CA: United Artists, 2008.

Scott, Jason, director. *BBS: The Documentary.* DVD. Cambridge, MA: Bovine Ignition Systems, 2005.

Skinner, W. F., and A. M. Fream. "A Social Learning Theory Analysis of Computer Crime among College Students." *Journal of Research in Crime and Delinquency* 34, no. 4 (1997): 495–518.

Sterling, Bruce. *The Hacker Crackdown: Law and Disorder on the Electronic Frontier.* New York: Bantam Books, 1992.

ThePirateBay.org. http://thepiratebay.org/.

ttol. "Operation Buccaneer Updates." http://free.hostultra.com/~parazite/scenebusts72.htm.

twixted. "Death Race DVDSCR(2008)." The Pirate Bay. http://thepiratebay.org/torrent/4403438/death_race_dvdscr(2008).

USA Today. "Peer-to-Peer Networks Unveil Code of Conduct." September 29, 2003, http://www.usatoday.com/tech/news/techpolicy/2003-09-29-p2p-code_x.htm.

U.S. Copyright Office. "Copyright and Digital Files." http://www.copyright.gov/help/faq/faq-digital.html.

U.S. Copyright Office. "Copyright Office Basics." http://www.copyright.gov/ circs/circ1.html.

U.S. Department of Justice. "NET Act: 17 U.S.C. and 18 U.S.C. as Amended (Redlined)." http://www.usdoj.gov/criminal/cybercrime/17-18red.htm.

U.S. Department of Justice. "Operation Buccaneer." Cybercrime.gov. http://www. cybercrime.gov/ob/OBMain.htm.

U.S. Department of Justice. "Twelve 'Operation Bandwidth' Software Pirates Enter into Group Guilty Plea (December 18, 2003)." http://www.usdoj. gov/criminal/cybercrime/bandwidthPlea.htm.

U.S. General Accounting Office. "The Use of Peer-to-Peer Networks to Access Pornography." http://www.gao.gov/new.items/d05634.pdf.

Varian, H. R. "Copying and Copyright." *Journal of Economic Perspectives* 19, no. 2 (2005): 121–38.

Vijayan, Jaikumar. "Harvard Professor Offers New Challenge to RIAA Antipiracy Campaign." *Computerworld Security*, October 30, 2008, http://www.com puterworld.com/action/article.do?command=viewArticleBasic&articleId= 9118599&source=NLT_PM&nlid=8.

Vijayan, Jaikumar. "Oregon: Ground Zero in Fight between RIAA, Alleged Music Pirates?" *Computerworld Security,* November 30, 2007, http://www.com puterworld.com/action/article.do?command=viewArticleBasic&articleId= 9050319.

Wake, Neil. "*Atlantic Recording Corporation, et al., vs. Pamela and Jeffrey Howell.*" http://www.ilrweb.com/viewILRPDF.asp?filename=atlantic_howell_ 080429Decision.

INDEX

A&M Records v. Napster, 133–35
Acceptable use policy (AUP), 22
Adware, 54
America On-Line (AOL), 23–24
Anti-P2P services, 64–65
Anti-virus protection, 66–67
ANts network, 141
AOHell, 23–24
Arista v. Does, 1–17, 145
ARPANET, 17
Assassin's guild BBS, 24
Atlantic v. Andersen, 129–32
Audible Magic, 61

Bandwidth, 33
Beckerman, Ray, 131
Berne Convention, 105
BigChampagne, 80–81
BitTorrent, 41–43, 72–74, 147–48,
    155–56, 175, 189
Blackburn, David, 93
Blacklisting software, 69, 126
Botnet, 54
Boxee, 148–49
Bulletin board system, 17–20, 107

Business Software Association
    (BSA), 4, 24, 83–85, 90–91
Butler, Max, 24

Capitol v. Thomas, 146
Chicago Area Computer Hobbyist's
    Exchange (CACHE), 17–18
Christensen, Ward, 17
Client-server model, 32–34
Client software, 39
Cloud, *See* Swarm
Cohen, Bram, 147–48
Comcast, 65
Compression, 47–48
Convenience samples, 83
Courier, 48
Copyright, history of, 101–10;
    protection in U.S. Constitution,
    104, 112; use of, 110–13
Copyright Act, 107, 110, 146
Copyright infringement, and theft,
    14, 90, 119; civil copyright
    infringement, 125–36;
    Congressional hearings,
    144; contributory copyright

Copyright infringement (*continued*)
infringement, 134; criminal
copyright infringement, 122–25;
statutory damages, 114, 145–46;
vicarious copyright infringement,
134
Cracker, 47
Cracking, 20
Cyberstrike, *See* Operation
cyberstrike
Cynosure BBS, 108

Danger Mouse, 113
Denial of Service (DoS), 64
Digital Millennium Copyright
Act, 109
Digital piracy. *See* Piracy
Digital rights management
(DRM), 139
Digital Theft Deterrence and
Copyright Damages Improvement
Act, 114, 115–16
DirectConnect (DC) network, 38
Distros, 48
Download ratios, 68
Drink or Die (DoD), 122–23

Electronic Frontier Foundation
(EFF), 101
Encoder, 47
Encryption, 143
Evaluating piracy research, 77–79

Fair use, 115–16
Fanning, Shawn, 11–12, 26–29
FastTrack network, 41, 135
Federal Communications
Commission (FCC), 65
Fell, John, 3
File Transfer Protocol (FTP),
22–23, 107
FXP, 48–49

Games, computer, 14, 19
Gates, Bill, 14–16

Gnutella network, 40, 61, 81, 125
Grey Album, 113
Gutenberg, Johann, 102

Hackers, 13, 34, 48, 142–43
Hacker ethic, 13
Higher Education Opportunity Act
(HEOA), 117–18
Hollinger, Richard, 82
Homebrew Computer Club,
12–17, 150
Hybrid P2P model, *See* Peer-to-Peer
(P2P) file sharing

Intellectual property, 3–4
Internet, 30
Internet relay chat (IRC), 22–23,
71, 107
Internet service provider (ISP), 31
IP address, 31, 58–59

Jobs, Steve, 16
Johns, Adrian, 3

KaZaA, 48–49, 63–64, 161

LaMacchia, David, 108
Leech, 41–42
Legal precedent, 111
Lessig, Lawrence, 119, 138
Levy, Steven, 13
Liebowitz, Stan, 91
LimeWire, 40, 81

Malware, 53–55
Mashups, 113
McQuade, Samuel, 88–89
MediaSentry, 58–63
MGM v. Grokster, 9, 135–36
Microsoft, 14–15, 24
Mininova, 80
MITS Altair BASIC, 14
Motion Picture Association of
America (MPAA), 4, 87, 94–95
MP3, 24–25

Napster, 11–12, 26–29, 37–38
Neeson, Charles, 146
No Electronic Theft (NET) Act, 108–9, 115, 124
Novell, 24

Oberholzer-Gee, Felix, and Koleman Strumpf, 91–93
Oikarinen, Jarkko, 22
Online piracy. *See* Piracy
Online piracy management services, 138
Operation bandwidth, 123–25
Operation buccaneer, 122–23
Operation cyberstrike, 24
Oregon State University, 145
Owner Free File System (OFF), 141

Packets, 31–32
Parents, 71–73
Peer-to-Peer (P2P) file sharing, 34–41; configuration of clients, 67; dangers of, 54–73; decentralization, 37; early adoption of, 27–28; effects on industry, 89–96; extent of, 75–89; hybrid P2P model, 34–38; identification of P2P users, 58–63; origins of available files, 43–49; overview of technology, 34–51; safe use, 65–71; search methods, 38, 40; true P2P model, 38–41; using P2P, 49–51
PeerGuardian, *See* Blacklisting software
Pew Internet and American Life Project, 85–86
Phreak, 21
Piracy: definitions, 4; of sheet music, 10; origin of, 3–4; types of pirate, 119
Pirate Bay, the, 79–80, 114, 143
Planning for lawsuits, 128–29
Pornography, 55–56
Printing press, 102–3
Prioritizing Resources and Organization for Intellectual

Property (PRO-IP) Act, 109–10, 115, 144
Private P2P networking, 142–44
Proxy, 143–44

Ransomware, 54
Razor1911, 122–23
Recording Industry Association of America (RIAA), 4, 25, 60–63, 68–72, 125–32, 138–42, 153, 184, 194
Relakks, 143
Reset packet, 65
Ritter, Jordan, 26
RogueWarriorz (RWZ), 123

Safe harbor provisions, 116
SafeNet, 64
Sandvine, 65, 81
Scene release, 44–45
Seed, 41
Settlements, 127
Seuss, Randy, 17–18
Shatnet FTP site, 123–25
SneakerNet, 17
Software publishers association (SPA), *See* Business Software Association (BSA)
Sonny Bono Copyright Term Extension Act, 109
Sony v. Tenenbaum, 146
Sony v. Universal, 135
Spoofing, 59, 63–64
Spyware, 54
Stakeholders, 5
Stationers' Guild, 10, 103
Statistics, extent of piracy, 97; movie piracy, 98; music piracy, 98; software piracy, 97
Statute of Anne, 103
Sting operations, 21, 24, 123–24
Strumpf, Koleman, *See* Felix Oberholzer-Gee
Subpoenas, 127, 145
Supplier, 45–46

Swarm, 41
Sysop, 19

Theft, 14, 90, 119
Throttling, 65
Topsites, 48
Transmission Control Protocol/
    Internet Protocol (TCP/IP), 30–32
True P2P model, *See* Peer-to-Peer
    (P2P) file sharing

Usenet, 70–71

Virus. *See* Malware

Warez scene, 20, 22–23, 43,
    122–25
WarGames, 21
Wozniak, Steve, 16

Xbox media center (XBMC), 149

ABOUT THE AUTHOR

NATHAN W. FISK is currently a doctoral student in the Science and Technology Studies program at Rensselaer Polytechnic Institute and an editorial assistant for the *Journal of Cultural Anthropology.* Over the past eight years, Fisk has worked on a variety of research projects and training workshops centered on fostering a better public understanding of youth computer crime and abuse, including the Rochester Cyber Safety and Ethics Initiative. Fisk has presented his research alongside Dr. Samuel McQuade at the Annual National Institute of Justice Conference and the Recording Industry Association of America headquarters, along with dozens of local school districts. His interest in online piracy and intellectual property springs from his experiences both with the computer underground and the warez scene and working with the information security office at the Rochester Institute of Technology—once known as the mother ship of online piracy in the United States.